SCROLL SAW
woodworking
& CRAFTS

WINTER2023 ■ ISSUE 93

51

14

DEPTS.

4 *Editor's Note*
6 *Letters to the Editor*
8 *Product Review*
9 *Coming Features*
10 *Makers Challenge*
71 *Ad Directory*

COVER

40+ Ornament Patterns
...14, 25, 33, 45, 55, 59, 72

Poinsettia Box ...61

Mini Log Cabin...70

Friendly Bear...27

Advent Calendar...17

Tractor Toy...19

PROJECTS

19 *Toy Tractor*
Whether you're a farmer or not, this sturdy build will provide years of play
By Brad Anderson

47 *Easy Hardwood Toolkit*
Have fun making this educational toy for the little handyperson in your life
By Rita Cels

51 *Intarsia Sports Car*
Capture the feeling of a road rally with this spirited classic convertible
By Janette Square

61 *Poinsettia Box*
Create a beautiful vessel with easy compound-cutting, wood veneer, and a little patience
By Carole Rothman

TECHNIQUES

39 *Santa and Sleigh Balance Toy*
A sleepy village and a snowman counterweight complete this charming Christmas Eve tableau
By Richard Packer

70 *Tiniest Cabin Construction Set*
Tiny homes are a trend these days, but this wee log cabin has them all beat
By Dave Van Ess

Search for Scroll Saw Woodworking & Crafts on Facebook, Pinterest, TikTok, and Instagram

PATTERNS

14 Fretwork Snowflakes
These lacy designs are striking as coasters or ornaments
By Jordan and Noelle Petersen

17 Horizontal Advent Calendar
This new take on a holiday classic features a movable tree
By Sue Mey

25 Intarsia Wreath
All you need to complete this beginner ornament are four little wood scraps
By Brad Eklund and Hazel Trinidad

27 Bear Lookout
This intermediate project uses negative space and strategically chosen frets to create the illusion of difficulty
By Charlie Dearing

29 Merry Christmas Sign
Scroll a festive freestanding sign or an appliqué for a backer of your choice
By Wayne and Jacob Fowler

31 Penguin Pileup
Stack these flightless birds several ways for a fun balancing game
By Jaeheon Yun

33 Dangle Critter Ornaments
This project combines simple shapes with beginner compound-cutting techniques
By Sue Mey

36 Piggy Bank
Easy to cut and construct, this functional project is a perfect way to introduce kids to the workshop
By Leonard Pick

45 Mid-Century Modern Ornaments
Elevate your tree décor with these classy, stylized baubles
By Frederick P. Arndt

55 Fretwork Candy Ornaments
Nostalgic decorations make a sweet treat for your tree this year
By Keith Fenton

57 Happy Hanukkah!
Celebrate the Festival of Lights with this trio of versatile patterns
By Wayne and Jacob Fowler

59 Easy Intarsia Snowman
All it takes to bring Frosty to life are a few small offcuts
By Brad Eklund and Hazel Trinidad

72 Layered Snowflake Ornaments
Contrasting woods add depth and body to these delicate designs
By Keith Fenton

FEATURE

68 Piece of Cake
Carole Rothman talks baking, box making, and the value of constant experimentation
By Kaylee Schofield

47

61

Find these free extras at
SCROLLSAWER.COM

Free Project – Want more ornaments? Use resin to add color to fretwork baubles by Clayton Meyers! (See the first few patterns in the pullout section.)

E-Newsletter – Get expert tips, techniques, and projects straight to your inbox between print issues of the magazine by signing up at scrollsawer.com/enews.

What It's All About

As soon as the first frosty night of the season hits, our eagerest neighbors break out the icicle lights and each grocery store chain trots out its own line of peppermint-flavored snacks. This change is sudden, and the sprint toward the holidays can seem even more so, making us hyperconscious of time and how to optimize it for both productivity and joy. The thing is, though, in our mad rush to master the gift-giving, get-togethers, and requisite feeling of winter magic, it's easy to forget about people in the process.

So before you jump into the projects in this issue—which, we assure you, are eclectic and fun—we want to invite you to participate in something cool. We're running an ornament scroll-off on scrollsawer.com. You can enter with any ornament you've made, from the magazine or otherwise. There are prizes, and you get to see what other scrollers are doing all around the world (more details on page 7). Who knows? Taking a minute away from the holiday bustle might just be the energizer you need to make this year's builds that much better.

Once you've filled that inspiration jar, spend it on a simple "toolkit" for the little woodworker in your life (page 47). If you favor more challenging projects, try a toy tractor with attachments for a wagon and harrow (page 19). Better yet, hone your skills on a tiny cabin construction set that'll test your mettle cutting 90° angles—no mean feat (page 70).

To venture outside the world of toys, check out three festive intarsia projects: a beginner wreath and snowman you can use as ornaments or magnets (pages 25 and 59), and a sweet sports car that's almost like unwrapping the real thing (page 51). Stack cut a treeful of ornaments featuring everything from snowflakes to candy to raccoons with dangly feet (pages 14, 72, 55, and 33). Or, forego the wrapping altogether and make the vessel the gift, with a meticulously crafted poinsettia box that combines compound-cutting with box-making techniques (page 61).

Once you're done toiling for the season and every coat of lacquer has dried, don't forget to show off what you've made—write us a letter, join our Scroll Saw Woodworking Group on Facebook, post to our forum, or sign up for a class at a local makerspace. It'll fuel your imagination, but better yet, you may just walk away with a new sense of community as a result.

Happy scrolling (and happy holidays)!

Kaylee Schofield, Editor
schofield@foxchapelpublishing.com

The Penguin Pileup (page 31) puzzle pieces make for a fun flat puzzle or stacking game.

Printed in the USA
Winter 2023
Volume 24, Number 4 (Issue No. 93)
Internet: Scrollsawer.com

Scroll Saw Woodworking & Crafts Magazine
903 Square Street, Mount Joy, PA 17552
Phone: 717-560-4703
editors@scrollsawer.com

Our Mission
To promote scrolling as an artform and an enjoyable pastime—for all ages and all skill levels.

Publisher/CEO . . . . Alan Giagnocavo
Editor . . . . Kaylee Schofield
Associate Editor . . . . Dorissa Bolinski
Editorial Administrator . . . . Kelly Umenhofer
Art Director . . . . Jon Deck
Social Media Manager . . . . Shane Speal
Contributing Photographer . . . . Mike Mihalo
Technical Illustrator . . . . Jon Deck

President/COO . . . . David Miller
Vice President, Acquisitions . . . . Erin Turner
Vice President, Sales . . . . Michele Sensenig
Vice President, IT Operations . . . . Paul Metzger

Customer Service for Subscribers
Visit scrollsawer.com, call 888-840-8590,
email customerservice@foxchapelpublishing.com,
or write *Scroll Saw Woodworking & Crafts*,
903 Square Street, Mount Joy, PA 17552.

Newsstand Distribution: Comag Marketing Group
Circulation Consultant: National Publisher Services
Printed by Fry Communications

©2023 by Fox Chapel Publishing Co. Inc.
All Rights Reserved. Printed in USA

Subscription Rates in US Dollars
One year $29.99
Two years $59.98

Canada
One year $34.99
Two years $69.98

International
One year $39.99
Two years $79.98

Display Advertising/Classifieds
For rates and/or a media kit, call Shane Speal at 800-457-9112 x156,
or email advertising@foxchapelpublishing.com.

Wholesale/Distribution
Scroll Saw Woodworking & Crafts is available to retailers for resale on
advantageous terms. Contact Fox Chapel Publishing Sales at
sales@foxchapelpublishing.com or 800-457-9112 (opt. #2).

Identification Statement: Scroll Saw Woodworking & Crafts, vol. 24, no. 4
(WINTER 2023) (ISSN#1532-5091) is published quarterly by
Fox Chapel Publishing Co. Inc., 903 Square Street, Mount Joy, PA 17552.
Periodicals postage paid at Lancaster, PA and additional mailing offices.
POSTMASTER: Send address changes to Scroll Saw Woodworking & Crafts,
903 Square Street, Mount Joy, PA 17552.

Publication Mail Agreement #40649125
Return Undeliverable Canadian Addresses to:
Station A, PO Box 54, Windsor, ON N9A 6J5
shannon@foxchapelpublishing.com.

Scrolling and the use of associated equipment can potentially result in health hazards and injuries. While we cannot impo[...]
standards in every article, we do ask that you make safety your number one priority. Protect your respiratory system, hearing,[...]
the rest of your body with the proper safety equipment and prudent precautions. Read manuals supplied with your tools. Be a[...]
accidents occur when you are tired or distracted. And when in doubt, seek advice from professionals on how to maintain ye[...]

Note to Professional Copy Services: *The publisher grants you permission to make up to ten copies for any purchaser of this magazine who states the copies are for personal use.*

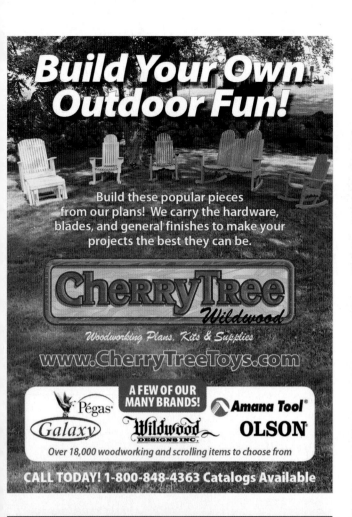

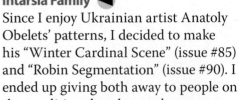

Intarsia Family

Since I enjoy Ukrainian artist Anatoly Obelets' patterns, I decided to make his "Winter Cardinal Scene" (issue #85) and "Robin Segmentation" (issue #90). I ended up giving both away to people on the condition that they make generous donations to benefit Ukrainian refugees. It is a great feeling when intarsia can help people around the world!

Chuck Miller *Lancaster, P*

Seaside Memories

My wife often chooses projects for me to scroll and came across Judy Gale Roberts' "Seaside Serenity" (issue #39). The piece was a great reminder of past trips and

travels to the beach. My wife helped me choose the types of exotic woods we would use for the project, which included Manitoba maple, sumac, poplar, and zebrawood. The Manitoba maple was one of the last pieces I had from my grandpa, who had created intarsia for decades.

Craig Boudreau *Petrolia, Ont.*

Scrolling Through Summer

I love your magazine and was inspired by Emily Lewis' "Animal Cracker Train" from the summer issue (#91) to make a coat rack for my great grandchildren. I am currently working through more magazine projects from the summer issue, including Brad Anderson's "Classic Car Toy."

Zina Hamminga *Nanaimo, B.C.*

Write to Us! *Tell us your thoughts on our projects, ideas for new patterns, scrolling experiences, and woodworking show stories. Write to us at: Letters to the Editor, Scroll Saw Woodworking & Crafts, 903 Square Street, Mount Joy, PA 17552 or email editors@scrollsawer.com. You can also send us your letters and photos via Instagram! Tag us @scrollsawwoodworking.*

Off to the Races

Scrolling and woodworking are both huge passions of mine, and I enjoy making any project I can. I decided to make Eric Van Malderen's "Porsche Puzzle" from issue #86 as a challenge. I ended up giving the puzzle away to a child I know.

Steve Romero *Orem, Utah*

SET IT STRAIGHT

The owl pattern on page 50 of issue #92 had a few tight frets around the beak. A modified version of this pattern is now available on the landing pages for the fall and winter issues.

One of the three patterns for Sue Mey's Easy Vases from the spring issue (#90) was omitted from the pattern pullout section. For the missing third pattern, visit scrollsawer.com. The pattern is included on the Spring 2023 (#90) landing page. We apologize for the errors.

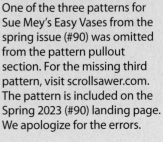

Seyco's *New* and *Improved* Scroller's Drill

Save time and tears drilling entry holes for a range of projects

By Staff of Scroll Saw Woodworking & Crafts

Drill with 10 bits: MSRP $139.00
Seyco.com

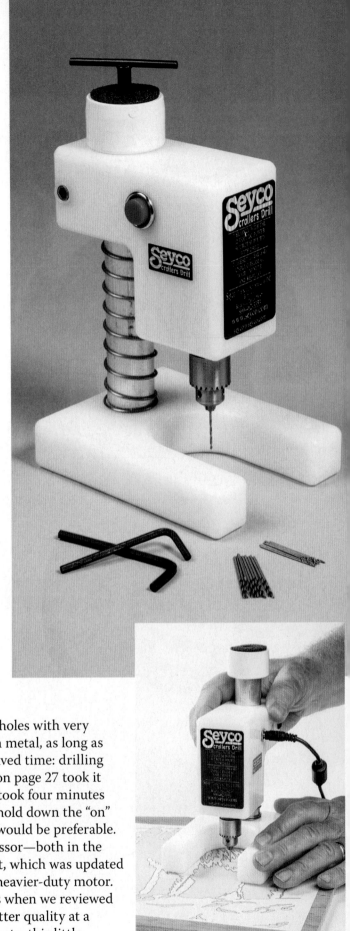

I f you've ever tackled a fretwork project of moderate to large scale, you know how tedious it can be to drill the entry holes. Not only that—depending on the size of your drill press, its throat depth may limit your ability to reach the center of the piece at all. (One of our staff has a small benchtop model at home, which can make prepping even 10" trivet blanks a near impossibility!) Seyco's scroller's drill, a new-and-improved version of the model we reviewed in spring 2010 (issue #38), is here to ease the process.

Small and compact, the drill differs from a standard drill press: instead of moving the workpiece around as you go, you slide the drill across the surface of the wood. The machine comes with a chuck key, DC power supply, and 10 small bits in popular sizes under ¹⁄₁₆" (2mm)—the typical threshold for most blade-entry holes. It does accommodate bits up to ⅛" (3mm)-diameter, but if you're using this size, Seyco recommends multiple plunges.

We tested this product on ⅛" (3mm) and ¼" (6mm) plywood, ½" (1.3cm) basswood and cherry, ¾" (1.9cm) walnut, and 1" (2.5cm) pine. None of these materials presented a challenge, and the machine produced clean holes with very little applied pressure. (It's also rated for plastic and thin metal, as long as you use the appropriate bit for the task.) The tool also saved time: drilling entry holes for Charlie Dearing's bear fretwork pattern on page 27 took it two minutes 23 seconds, whereas a standard drill press took four minutes 25 seconds. One small annoyance is that the user must hold down the "on" button while plunging the bit; a standard on/off switch would be preferable.

The new model is easier to maneuver than its predecessor—both in the shape of the motor housing and the mobility of the shaft, which was updated for greater drilling stability. The machine also boasts a heavier-duty motor.

Amazingly, the latest model is $10 cheaper than it was when we reviewed the earlier version in 2010—so you're literally getting better quality at a lower price. If fretwork or production cutting are your forte, this little powerhouse will quickly become a staple in your shop.

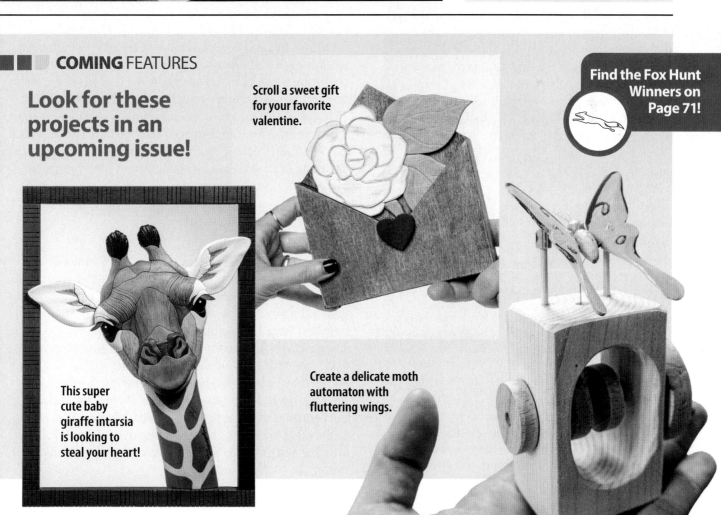

■ ■ **COMING** FEATURES

Look for these projects in an upcoming issue!

Scroll a sweet gift for your favorite valentine.

This super cute baby giraffe intarsia is looking to steal your heart!

Create a delicate moth automaton with fluttering wings.

Find the Fox Hunt Winners on Page 71!

This past June, we partnered with Makers Challenge Central for their 2023 Scroll Saw-Themed Challenge. Scrollers had three weeks to create a piece around the theme of "Big Food," a food-inspired project with super-sized dimensions. At the end of the three weeks, dozens of scrollers showed off their intricate and delicious pieces in the form of sawdust-encrusted blueberry muffins, fairy fruit houses, tacos as big as Texas, and more! Check out some of the contestants below and see what creations they whipped up with their scroll saws. Be sure to stay tuned for our upcoming *SSW&C* challenges: Ornament Scroll-Off, Favorite Fretwork Challenge, and Home Décor Challenge.

Jennifer Hine *Wichita, Kan.* ▲

For Jennifer Hine, the possibilities are endless when it comes to what she can create on the scroll saw. When she heard about the Scroll Saw Challenge, Jennifer kept that same mindset and branched out into creating something totally new to her—a tray of giant blueberry muffins! "This challenge was a lot of fun and I enjoyed having full creative freedom while creating such a massive piece," she said. After 25 hours of cutting, shaping, and painting by hand, Jennifer transformed a few simple pieces of wood into a rustic "metal" tray filled with realistic muffins that look good enough to eat. See more of Jennifer's work on Instagram @elegantquirk.

◀

Laura Kacir *Yoakum, Texas*

Even with temperatures reaching over 100°F in Texas, Laura Kacir was determined to create her piece—a large margarita, and tacos inside a cutout of the Lone Star State—for the Scroll Saw Challenge. "Since everything is bigger in Texas, I knew this piece had to be bigger, too," she said. With her "don't tell me I can't, because I'll prove that I can" attitude, Laura got to work cutting, layering, and shaping during the day and airbrushing the piece in the evening after temperatures went down. Even though the contest is over, Laura is working on adding a backlight to the piece and hopes to have it displayed in her favorite little bar and grill in town. See more of Laura's work on Instagram @lollipopskreations.

For more information on upcoming challenges, visit makerschallengecentral.com or scrollsawer.com.

Jess Paris *Akron, Ohio*
Jess Paris' piece embodies the phrase "art imitating life": she came across the challenge while eating at a ramen shop. "I had considered other foods, such as donuts and pizza, but felt ramen would give me more of a challenge with all the different elements in each bowl," she said. Even though this is her first time scrolling a ramen bowl, she has also created other food-related pieces, such as ice cream sundaes, ballpark hot dogs, and exotic mushrooms. After her piece was finished, Jess sold it to a couple in Chicago, who wanted to commemorate their monthly ramen dinner dates. See more of Jess' work on Instagram @jparisdesigns.

Bri Harvey *Marion, Ill.* ▶
Bri Harvey has always loved woodworking and fantasy. When she heard of the Scroll Saw Challenge, she knew just how to combine these passions: scrolling giant fairy houses shaped like fruits. After finishing up her design, Bri spent days scrolling and shaping the pieces before painting each one by hand, including the forest background. "This challenge really let me flex my creative muscle from start to finish because I wasn't just replicating a photo but creating something from scratch," she said. Once the piece was finished, Bri decided to hang it in her shop in memory of her 13-year-old dachshund Marley, who passed away while she was constructing the piece. See more of Bri's work on Instagram @maplemoonco.

Darbi McGee *Denver, Colo.*
As soon as she came across the Scroll Saw Challenge, Darbi McGee instantly had a sweet idea for what she could scroll—a giant waffle. Inspired by her three daughters' love of the breakfast food, Darbi wanted to design her waffle to be three-dimensional and decided to add layers to the piece. "I wanted to do something outside my comfort zone and think BIG!" she said. Darbi also cut smaller pieces of fruit (strawberries, blueberries, and banana slices), chocolate chips, a pat of butter, and made syrup from a mixture of glue and dye to top off her culinary cutout. See more of Darbi's work on Instagram @redrovergifts.

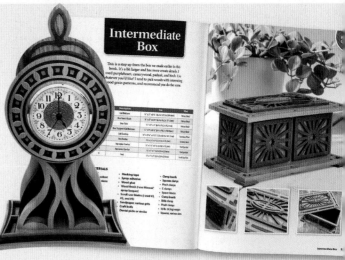

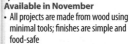

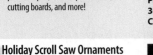
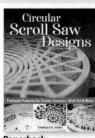

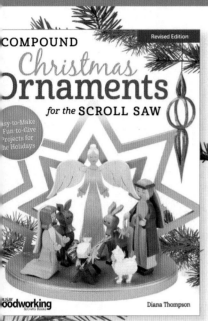

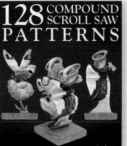

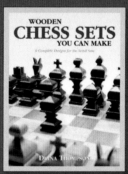

Fretwork Snowflakes

These lacy designs are striking as coasters or ornaments

By Jordan and Noelle Petersen

When I first started scrolling eight years ago, I used patterns from books, but it wasn't long before I wanted to make something unique and individual. I began cutting out paper snowflakes and sticking them to wood to cut on the scroll saw. As my skill progressed, I learned to use design software to digitally create more intricate patterns. I also began experimenting with glued-up scraps for a variety of interesting looks. The snowflakes for this article are made from cherry, hackberry, and walnut, and the striped one is made from assorted hardwoods.

Getting Started

Sand the blank with 120-grit sandpaper and remove excess dust with a cloth or compressed air. Cover the blank with blue painter's tape or packaging tape on the side you want to cut. Print out the paper pattern and cut it out close to the edges so that you have the clearest view of where to place the pattern on the prepared wood. Attach the pattern to the blank with repositionable spray adhesive, and then carefully smooth it out.

Note: For my striped snowflakes, I edge-glue different strips of contrasting wood until I form a piece of wood that's at least 4½" (11.4cm) square. Then I let the glue dry thoroughly and attach the patterns in the manner described above.

Cutting and Drilling

Carefully drill blade-entry holes with a ⅟₃₂" (1mm)-dia. bit. For cutting the frets on all snowflakes, I use either a #1 or #3 Flying Dutchman ultra-reverse blade. Start by cutting all the inside areas of the pattern, and then cut the perimeter. Once the shape is completely cut, remove the tape and pattern by gently peeling it off the wood.

Sanding and Finishing

Sand the snowflakes with 120-grit sandpaper to start, and work through the grits up to at least 320. You can either hand-sand the snowflakes or use an orbital sander, but take care to avoid breakage. After sanding, remove the dust using either a compressor or a can of compressed air.

Finish the snowflakes with thinned wipe-on poly or tung oil by dipping them in the finish and immediately hanging them on a drying rack. After allowing five to ten minutes for excess finish to drip off, wipe the snowflakes with a lint-free rag to remove excess. The snowflakes then immediately go back onto the drying rack to finish drying. Repeat this process as many times as desired to obtain a sheen you like. I do a minimum of two coats. Let dry for 24 hours.

Materials & Tools

Materials
- Wood, such as cherry, hackberry, and walnut, ¼" (6mm) thick: 4½" (11.4cm) square
- Tape: painter's or packaging
- Glue, such as Tite Bond: wood or white
- Spray adhesive: repositionable
- Sandpaper: 120- to 320-grit
- Can of compressed air
- Finish, such as wipe-on poly or tung oil
- Lint-free rag

Tools
- Scroll saw with blades: #1 or #3 Flying Dutchman ultra-reverse
- Sander: orbital (optional)
- Air compressor (optional)
- Paintbrush
- Drying rack
- Drip tray

The author used these products for the project. Substitute your choice of brands, tools, and materials as desired.

Sourcing Hardwoods

I obtain wood from a variety of local sources, like hardwood stores or sawmills. Some of the wood I use is scrap from cabinet shops. I also gather large quantities of windfallen wood and use my band saw to cut up tree branches I find. This has allowed me to procure many species of wood—like pear, crabapple, catalpa, mulberry, hackberry, and locust—that are not typically available in stores. Sourcing wood this way helps me keep costs down. It's also nice to know that part of these trees will live on as beautiful items in people's homes.

Fretwork Snowflakes Patterns

Jordan Petersen is a scroll saw enthusiast from Nebraska. He and his wife, Noelle, both enjoy woodworking and designing different patterns for the scroll saw, as well as sewing and many other crafting pursuits. You can find Jordan on Instagram @jordanpetersen85 and on Instagram and Etsy @jnadoptionshop.

HORIZONTAL
Advent
Calendar

This new take on a holiday classic features a movable tree

By Sue Mey
Cut by Joe Pascucci

People have long used Advent calendars to check off the 24 days leading to Christmas. Classic Advent calendars have little doors that open to reveal a small treat, such as a Bible verse, toy, or piece of chocolate. This Advent calendar is a more streamlined way to count down the days. The tree is moved from one opening to the next as December progresses, and can be displayed on a tabletop or mantel.

Prepping and Cutting

Apply masking tape or painter's tape to the blanks for the four base pieces, the tree, and the numbers. Photocopy the patterns and apply spray adhesive or a glue stick to the backs. Press the patterns in place on the wood, smoothing out any air bubbles. Cut the stand pieces on a scroll saw. Then drill blade entry holes for the tree and numbers and cut those items out, as well.

1234567890

Assembling and Finishing

Sand the workpieces by hand until you have achieved a smooth finish, working progressively through the grits to 320. Remove all the sanding dust with a clean cloth, using a hard-bristled paintbrush for tight areas.

Using an artist's small flat brush, paint the tree with green acrylic or spray paint, depending on your preference. Then add color to the star and paint the front and side surfaces of the numbers.

Working on a level surface, glue the four horizontal pieces together one by one, starting with the three shorter segments followed by the longer one. Clamp each section and let the assembly dry between additions.

Apply wood stain to the stand, if desired, and allow it to dry. Glue the numbers onto the horizontal piece with wood glue, staying below the open squares. To ensure the numbers are in a straight line, apply a strip of masking tape from left to right as a guideline. Remove the tape when you are done. Finish the project with several thin coats of clear spray varnish, allowing each coat to dry before applying the next.

Horizontal Advent Calendar Patterns

Additional patterns for the *HORIZONTAL ADVENT CALENDAR* are in the pullout section.

Materials & Tools

Materials
- Wood, such as pine, ¾" (1.9cm) thick: stand Part 1, 1¾" x 12⁹⁄₁₆" (4.4cm x 32cm)
- Wood, such as pine, ¾" (1.9cm) thick: stand Part 2, 3 each 1¾" x 10⅝" (4.4cm x 27cm)
- Wood, such as pine, ¾" (1.9cm) thick: tree, 4¹⁄₁₆" x 6¹⁄₁₆" (10.3cm x 15.4cm)
- Wood, such as Baltic birch plywood, ⅛" (3mm) thick: numbers, 3 each 1" x 10" (2.5cm x 25.4cm) long
- Tape: masking, painter's (optional)
- Spray adhesive or glue stick
- Sandpaper: assorted grits to 320
- Clean cloth
- Acrylic or spray paints: green, gold, red

- Wood stain (optional)
- Wood glue
- Finish, such as clear satin spray varnish

Tools
- Scroll saw with blades: #3 and #7 reverse-tooth
- Drill press with bits: ¹⁄₁₆" (2mm)-dia., ⅛" (3mm)-dia.
- Paintbrushes: stiff-bristled and small flat
- Clamps

The author used these products for the project. Substitute your choice of brands, tools, and materials as desired.

Sue Mey lives in Pretoria, South Africa. To see more of her work, including a wide variety of patterns and pattern-making tutorials available for purchase, visit scrollsawartist.com. She can be contacted at suem@storage.co.za. Her pattern book, Lighted Scroll Saw Projects, *is available from schifferbooks.com and other outlets.*

Joe Pascucci started scrolling nearly 30 years ago. He also enjoys woodturning and other types of woodworking. Joe is a retired police sergeant and construction superintendent, and is the founding president of the Long Island Scroll Saw Association. When Joe's not in the woodshop, he can be found gardening, traveling, and spending time with his grandkids. To see more of Joe's work, visit the Members section of liwoodworkers.org.

Toy Tractor

Whether you're a farmer or not, this sturdy build will provide years of play

By Brad Anderson

I enjoy making toys that children can play with for generations. This tractor features a small, sturdy frame with wheels that allow it to move around on various surfaces. It also comes with a detachable trailer and a harrow. Playing with a toy tractor can be a fun way for children to explore their imaginations and learn about farming. It can also help develop their motor skills and hand-eye coordination as they move the toy around.

Getting Started

I used leftover wood—which happened to be cherry and oak—for this project. Cut blanks to manageable sizes for all the components of the tractor. For the engine, glue together two pieces of the ¾" (1.9cm) wood, and then clamp until dry. Next, cover the blanks with painter's tape and use spray adhesive to glue the patterns to their surfaces.

You could also leave the tractor natural and swap the wagon for a harrow.

Use a scroll saw with a #7 skip-tooth blade to cut out the pieces for the tractor, harrow, and wagon. The tractor side and fender pieces should be stack-cut so they mirror each other. The parts will be assembled in order, so group the cut pieces for each part of the vehicle together to keep them from getting mixed up.

1 Prepare the sides, chassis, and fenders. Note the location of the holes on the patterns. Drill a 5/16" (8mm)-dia. hole in the chassis. Drill the holes in the front axle, which are 1/4" (6mm)-dia. on the face and 7/32" (5.6mm)-dia. on the ends. Then drill the 11/32" (9mm)-dia. holes in the sides and the 1/4" (6mm)-dia. holes in the seat bottom.

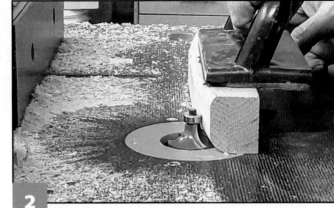

2 Form the engine. Cut the two pieces on the scroll saw, angling the table or arm as indicated in the patterns. Wipe off excess dust with a cloth, and glue and clamp the pieces. Let dry. Sand the faces smooth, and use a router or a pneumatic drum sander to round over the top edges.

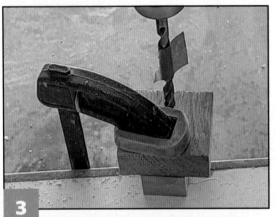

3 Make the seat. Glue the seat bottom and seat back together, and clamp until dry. When dry, glue the seat to the seat base on the chassis. Use the holes in the seat base as a guide and drill the holes to 1¼" (3.2cm) deep. Cut ¼" (6mm) dowels and insert them into the holes. Sand the dowels flush with the base.

4 Assemble the tractor body. Sand all parts to 150-grit. Smooth all inside edges. Use a ¼" (6mm) roundover bit or a belt sander to soften the edges of the roof. Glue the seat base assembly and sides to the chassis. The back of the sides and seat base should line up with the back points on the chassis. Glue the roof to the sides. Clamp all parts together so they don't shift while drying, and let dry completely before proceeding.

5 Attach the axle. When the tractor body is dry, use the sides as a guide and drill 11/32" (9mm)-dia. holes into the chassis, 1¼" (3.2mm) deep. Glue the front axle onto the chassis. Set the axle back ¼" (6mm) from the front edge of the chassis and center it. Using the holes in the axle as a guide, drill holes 1¼" (3.2cm) deep. Insert the dowels and sand them flush.

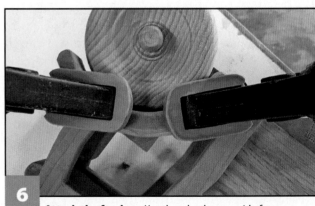

6 Attach the fenders. Use the wheels as a guide for placement; fenders should extend past the back of the sides and sit flush with the bottom of the sides. There will be about a ⅛" (3mm) gap between the fender and the wheel. Glue and clamp the fenders onto the sides.

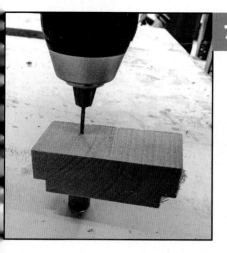

7   **Make the exhaust stack.** Cut a ½" (1.3cm) dowel 1½" (3.8cm) long and a ⁵⁄₁₆" (8mm) dowel 1¼" (3.2cm) long. Use a hand plane or sander to create a flat end on the ½" (1.3cm) dowel. Drill a ⁵⁄₁₆" (8mm) hole ⅜" (1cm) deep at the end of the ½" (1.3cm) dowel. Glue the ⁵⁄₁₆" (8mm) dowel into the ½" (1.3cm)-dia. dowel. Then glue this assembly to the right side of the tractor. *Note: You can drill a ½" (1.3cm) hole partway through a piece of scrap and drill a pilot hole in the center. This can be used to mark the center of the ½" (1.3cm) dowel to drill.*

Toy Tractor Patterns

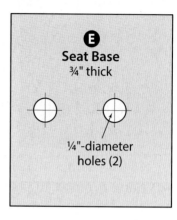

E

Seat Base
¾" thick

¼"-diameter holes (2)

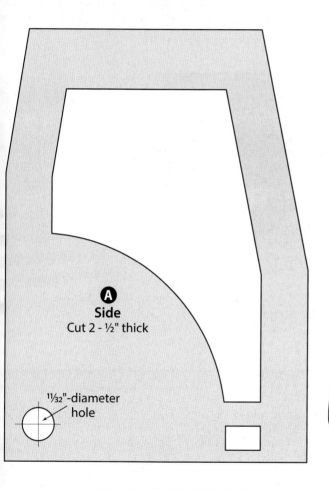

A

Side
Cut 2 - ½" thick

¹¹⁄₃₂"-diameter hole

D

Engine
Cut 2 - ¾" thick

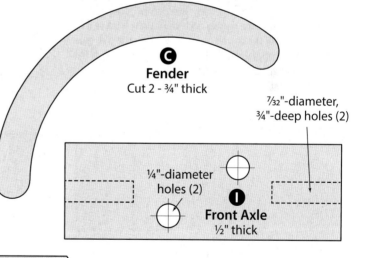

C

Fender
Cut 2 - ¾" thick

⁷⁄₃₂"-diameter, ¾"-deep holes (2)

¼"-diameter holes (2)

I

Front Axle
½" thick

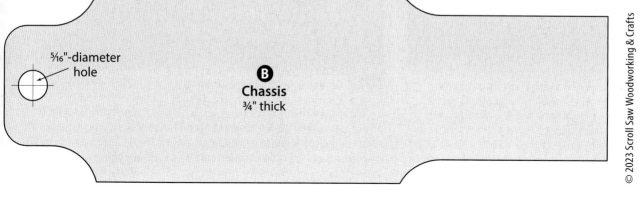

⁵⁄₁₆"-diameter hole

B

Chassis
¾" thick

MAKING THE HARROW

8 **Prepare the harrow.** Referring to the pattern, drill the ⅜" (1cm) and ¼" (6mm) harrow hitch holes in the top and ⅜" (1cm) and ⁵⁄₁₆" (8mm)-dia. holes in the harrow sides. Cut two pieces of ⅜" (1cm) dowel 4 ¾" (12.1cm) long and one piece of ¼" (6mm) dowel 5⅞" (15cm) long.

9 **Assemble the harrow.** Glue two ⅜" (1cm) dowels into one side of the harrow. Slide the harrow hitch so it is in the middle of the dowels and use cyanoacrylate (CA) glue to affix it into place. Glue the other side to the ends of the dowels. Let this assembly dry thoroughly, and then sand to smooth and soften all edges.

Toy Harrow Patterns

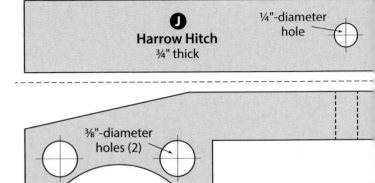

J Harrow Hitch
¾" thick

¼"-diameter hole

⅜"-diameter holes (2)

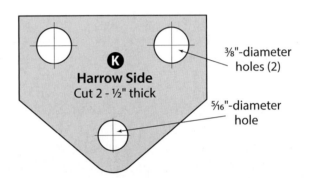

K Harrow Side
Cut 2 - ½" thick

⅜"-diameter holes (2)

⁵⁄₁₆"-diameter hole

MAKING THE WAGON

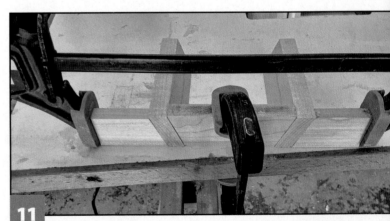

10 **Prepare the wagon.** Use a table saw to cut a 20° angle on both sides of the wagon. Then cut a 20° angle on each end of the wagon front. Alternatively, you could make the angled cut with a scroll saw, tilting the arm or table to 20°. Drill ⁷⁄₃₂" (5.6mm)-dia. holes at each end of the wagon's axle. Drill a ¼" (6mm)-dia. hole in the hitch blank.

11 **Glue up the wagon.** Glue the sides, front, and bottom together. Start by gluing the front to the bottom and clamp them together. Then glue the sides on. Clamp the sides to the front using some scraps cut at a 20° angle. Then clamp the sides to the bottom. When this assembly is completely dry, center the axle on the bottom and glue it to that piece. Center the hitch on the front of the wagon flush to the top and glue both pieces in place.

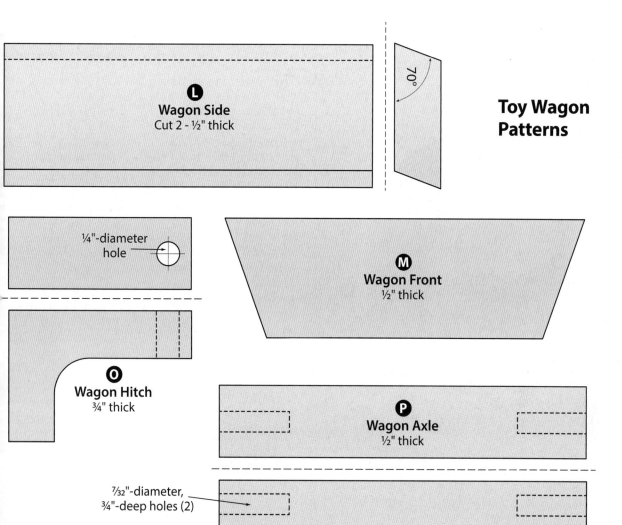

L
Wagon Side
Cut 2 - ½" thick

70°

Toy Wagon Patterns

¼"-diameter hole

M
Wagon Front
½" thick

O
Wagon Hitch
¾" thick

P
Wagon Axle
½" thick

⁷⁄₃₂"-diameter, ¾"-deep holes (2)

Assembling and Finishing

Sand all pieces to 150-grit. You can leave this project completely natural or finish in several ways; if you do choose to finish the project, do so before assembling. I like the natural look of wood, so I typically apply a clear coat of shellac, since it is child-safe. If you prefer a colorful tractor, use child-safe acrylic paints. Consider letting your child help paint the pieces. Painting is a safe way to involve kids in the workshop.

When all the pieces are completely dry, assemble the tractor, harrow, and wagon. Attach the 2¾" (7cm)-dia. wheels to the rear of the tractor and 1½" (3.8cm)-dia. wheels to the front of the tractor using axle pegs and glue.

To make the harrow, attach one 1½" (3.8cm)-dia. wheel to the end of the ¼" (6mm) dowel from step 8. Run this through the hole on the harrow, and then put four 1½" (3.8cm) wheels on the dowel before running it through the other end. Glue a 1½" (3.8cm) wheel onto the other side of the harrow. Space the wheels evenly on the dowel and glue them into place. I used cyanoacrylate (CA) glue for the

middle four wheels. *Tip: I lightly sanded the middle of the ¼" (6mm) dowel so the wheels move freely.*

Attach the 1½" (3.8cm)-dia. wheels to the wagon with axle pegs and glue. Finish by attaching the wheels to the wagon with axle pegs. Insert ¼" (6mm) dowels in the harrow and wagon hitch.

Tractor Assembly Drawing

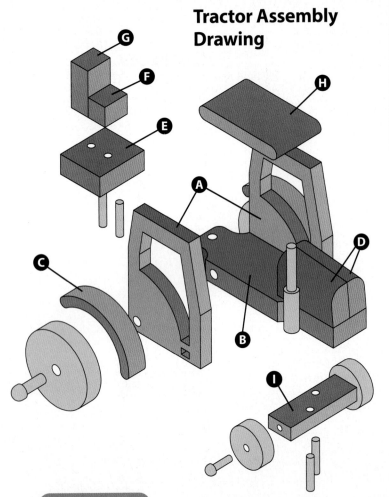

Parts List

	Part	Quantity	Materials	Dimensions	Presentation
A	Tractor Sides	2	Cherry, ½" (1.3cm)	3¼ x 4½ (8.3cm x 11.4cm)	Pattern
B	Chassis	1	Oak, ¾" (1.9cm)	2" x 6½" (5.1cm x 16.5cm)	Pattern
C	Fender	2	Oak, ¾" (1.9cm)	2⅛" x 3⅛" (5.4cm x 7.9cm)	Pattern
D	Engine	2	Oak, ¾" (1.9cm)	1½" x 2½" (3.8cm x 6.4cm)	Pattern
E	Seat Base	1	Oak, ¾" (1.9cm)	1¾" x 2" (4.4cm x 5.1cm)	Pattern
F	Seat Bottom	1	Oak, ¾" (1.9cm)	¾" x 1" (1.9cm x 2.5cm)	Dimensions
G	Seat Back	1	Oak, ¾" (1.9cm)	1" x 1¾" (2.5cm x 4.4cm)	Dimensions
H	Roof	1	Cherry, ½" (1.3cm)	2" x 3½" (5.1cm x 8.9cm)	Dimensions
I	Front Axle	1	Cherry, ½" (1.3cm)	1" x 3" (2.5cm x 7.6cm)	Pattern
J	Harrow Hitch	1	Cherry, ¾" (1.9cm)	1" x 3¾" (2.5cm x 9.5cm)	Pattern
K	Harrow Sides	2	Cherry, ½" (1.3cm)	1¼" x 2" (3.2cm x 5.1cm)	Pattern
L	Wagon Sides	2	Cherry, ½" (1.3cm)	1¼ x 4" (3.2cm x 10.2cm)	Pattern
M	Wagon Front	1	Cherry, ½" (1.3cm)	1¼" x 3²⁹⁄₃₂" (3.2cm x 9.9cm)	Pattern
N	Wagon Bottom	1	Cherry, ½" (1.3cm)	4" (10.2cm) square	Dimensions
O	Wagon Hitch	1	Cherry, ¾" (1.9cm)	1⅜" x 2" (3.5cm x 5.1cm)	Pattern
P	Wagon Axle	1	Cherry, ½" (1.3cm)	¾" x 4" (1.9cm x 10.2cm)	Pattern

Brad Anderson has been a hobbyist woodworker for about 20 years. He started designing and building furniture, but quickly ran out of room for all of it. Then about seven years ago, he started making and designing wooden toys for his children. See more of Brad's work and other plans on his Etsy page at AllNaturalToyPlans.

Intarsia Wreath

All you need to complete this beginner ornament are four little wood scraps

By Brad Eklund and Hazel Trinidad

I have fond memories of growing up in Maine, where my family made wreaths from balsam fir for a local company during the holidays. The scent of balsam fir always reminds me of childhood Christmastimes, with snowy landscapes and fun around every corner. That time of the year had a magical feeling, which continues with my kids and younger family members. We hope you capture some holiday magic when making this intarsia wreath.

Getting Started

Make four copies of the pattern: one for each type of wood and a master copy for reference. Apply the patterns to their respective pieces of wood with repositionable spray adhesive, and then drill an entry hole in the center.

Cutting

Note: As an alternate to cutting, the circles could be drilled out with a ½" (1.3cm)-dia. bit, then filled with ½" (1.3cm)-dia. dowels, about 9/16" (1.4cm) in length, rounded at the top ends, then painted. Cutting the project is straightforward. Leave the red bow segments all together until the bow fits perfectly in the wreath. Once all segments have been cut and adjusted, it's time to start shaping.

Shaping

All segments should be kept at approximately the same thickness. Slightly round over each segment edge of the ribbon with 220-grit sandpaper. Round over the yellow segments to give them a spherical appearance, and then round all edges of the wreath part. Use a rotary tool with a ¼" (6mm) sanding drum to round the exterior edges a bit more than the interior. Finish-sand everything to 220-grit.

Assembling and Finishing

If you want to stain or paint any piece, do so now. We like to use General Finishes green dye for the wreath, but if your piece of poplar is particularly green, dye may not be needed. After the paint or stain dries, check that everything still fits together well, as the wood can sometimes expand. Sand appropriately if any parts have expanded.

Glue all the segments together and let dry fully. Glue the intarsia onto your backing material, and then trace-cut along the exterior. Glue the backing onto the wreath. Drill a blade entry hole in the center of the backing and cut it out. *Note: Alternatively, you could trace the outline of the wreath and center hole on the backing material and cut the backer by itself, staying just inside the line.*

Touch up any paint or stain spots that you might have nicked with the blade while cutting the backing. Apply a clear satin lacquer and let dry thoroughly. Attach a screw eye and string, and you're all finished!

Intarsia Wreath Pattern

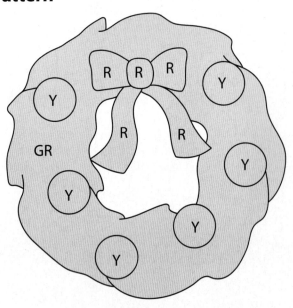

R .... Red wood such as redheart or padauk
Y .... Yellow wood such as yellowheart
GR .... Green dyed wood such as poplar

Materials & Tools

Materials
- Red wood, such as redheart or padauk, ½" (1.3cm) thick: ribbon, 1¼" (3.2cm) square
- Yellow wood, such as yellowheart, ½" (1.3cm) thick: balls, 6 each ½" (1.3cm) square
- Wood, such as poplar, ½" (1.3cm) thick: wreath, 3" (7.6cm) square
- Tempered hardboard, ⅛" (3mm) thick: backer, approx. 3" (7.6cm) square
- Spray adhesive: repositionable
- Sandpaper: 220-grit
- Tack cloth
- Lacquer: clear satin

- Wood glue
- Dye, such as General Finishes: green (optional)
- Screw eye (optional)
- Decorative string (optional)

Tools
- Scroll saw with blades: #5 MGT
- Drill with bit: ⅛" (3mm)-dia.
- Sander: belt
- Rotary tool with bit: ¼" (6mm) sanding drum

The author used these products for the project. Substitute your choice of brands, tools, and materials as desired.

Brad Eklund and Hazel Trinidad have been creating scroll saw art for the last seven years. They have always been fascinated by the beauty and intricacies of wildlife and nature in general. Brad has a degree in horticulture, while Hazel has a degree in wildlife. They live and work next to a nature preserve in coastal North Carolina. Find more of their work on Etsy at EntwoodDesigns.

Bear Lookout

This intermediate project uses negative space and strategic frets to create the illusion of difficulty

By Charlie Dearing

W hile the bear in this portrait is confidently surveying its territory, most bears spend all or part of the winter in hibernation—a low-level sleep state that allows them to go months without needing to eat or drink. Cut this project and you can keep it out all year, even as the real thing is napping. I've kept the frets fairly large, and replaced full cutouts with kerf details in some places so you don't need to remove as much wood. Take your time and have fun!

Getting Started

Apply the pattern to the surface of the wood. I prefer to tape down one side of the pattern (so it doesn't move around). Then trace it on with carbon paper and a pencil, but you can use repositionable spray adhesive, if desired. If you choose the former method, you'll need to sand away any remaining lines later. If you choose to stack cut, make the stack now, attaching the pieces with wire brads in the waste areas (or by binding the sides with packaging tape).

Drill the blade-entry holes. Since many of the pieces I cut have lots of frets, I use a scroller's drill from Seyco (see page 8 for a product review), as it doesn't have the same throat depth limitations as a traditional drill press. Then lightly sand the back of the piece with an orbital sander to remove the "blowouts" created by the holes, allowing you to maneuver your workpiece smoothly along the scroll saw table.

Cutting

Scroll the piece, starting with the interior cuts. The order in which you cut these frets is your call, but I typically start with the face of the subject. I start here because the face is the most important part; if I mess this up, I can start over without sinking too much time into the project. Once the frets are cut, cut the perimeter.

Sanding and Finishing

If you applied the pattern with spray adhesive, carefully remove it now. Hand-sand the surface with 180- and then 220-grit sandpaper; I often place the large waste areas back into place for added stability while sanding. Advanced scrollers could use an orbital sander here, but beginners should sand by hand depending on their comfort level to avoid breaking any delicate areas. Use needle files to clean out the fuzzies from the smaller frets.

Finish as desired; I applied a few light coats of semigloss spray lacquer, hand-sanding between coats. Once the finish is dry, add the backer; this can be cut from a contrasting wood, such as tempered hardboard or walnut, or from the same material as the main project with a coat or two of contrasting stain. Either secure both pieces in a frame or glue the backer to the portrait. Display as desired.

TIP

BOTTOM-FEEDING

After drilling the blade-entry holes, I often flip the piece over and widen each one with an awl, moving in circular motions. Since I feed the blade in through the bottom, this helps to limit the time it takes to find each hole by feel.

WANT MORE FRETWORK?

Wildlife Portraits in Wood
By Charles Dearing

Item 3386. Available for $14.95 plus S&H (parcel post) from Fox Chapel Publishing, FoxChapelPublishing.com, 800-457-9112, or your local retailer.

Materials & Tools

Materials
- Baltic birch plywood, ⅛" (3mm) thick: 8" x 10" (20.3cm x 25.4cm)
- Backing material, ¹⁄₁₆" (2mm) thick: sized for pattern
- Carbon transfer paper (optional)
- Pencil (optional)
- Spray adhesive: repositionable
- Sandpaper: assorted grits to 220
- Tape: clear packaging
- Finish, such as semigloss spray lacquer
- Glue: wood
- Oil-based stain (optional)

Tools
- Scroll saw with blades: #3 and #5 spiral
- Drill press or scroller's drill with bit: ¹⁄₁₆" (2mm)-dia.
- Sander: orbital (optional)
- Brad nailer with wire brads (optional)
- Needle files
- Awl (optional)

The author used these products for the project. Substitute your choice of brands, tools, and materials as desired.

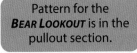

Pattern for the **BEAR LOOKOUT** is in the pullout section.

Charlie Dearing's artistic talents were evident at an early age, but he didn't discover the joys of scrolling until later in life. Scrolling became his passion, so Charlie started creating his own designs when he couldn't find commercial patterns to meet his needs. Find more of Charlie's work on his website, woodenvisions.com.

Merry Christmas Sign

Scroll a festive freestanding sign or an appliqué for a backer of your choice

By Wayne Fowler
Design by Jacob Fowler

I participate in many craft shows at Christmastime. One item that sells particularly well is a simple freestanding "Merry Christmas" sign that my son, Jacob, designed several years ago. When I mentioned this to him recently, he surprised me with many new versions of the holiday phrase, including the two in this project. Both signs can be cut as freestanding decorations, or you could make either as an applique and attach it to an attractive block of wood.

Getting Started

Photocopy the pattern you wish to cut. Cover the wood with clear packaging tape, and then attach the pattern to the tape with spray adhesive. The clear tape lets you see the wood underneath so you can properly place the pattern. It also helps to lubricate the blade while you are cutting and allows for quicker pattern removal when you are done.

Drill the blade-entry holes in the waste areas where the interior cuts will be made. You can use a larger drill bit for the larger space, which makes it easier to feed the blade through. Some of the smaller holes (such as those in the lettering) require a finer drill bit, however.

Stand-Alone Wordart

The Merry Christmas pattern with the snowflake has a base and should be cut from either a ¾" (1.9cm)-thick piece of maple or cherry so it can stand on its own. The simpler pattern will stand on its own if cut from thick-enough wood, or it can be cut from ¼" (6mm)-thick wood to be used as an applique on a backer. Cutting the signs using maple or cherry gives this project a nice rich color.

Cutting

Cut the project on a scroll saw, starting with the interior cuts. The size of the blade needed will depend on the wood thickness and density, as well as the level of detail in the cut. For most of these pieces, a #3 reverse-tooth blade will suffice. But for the smaller cuts such as those in the lettering, it may be better to use a #1 blade. When done with the internal frets, cut the perimeter of the piece.

Sanding and Finishing

I usually hand-sand the back of the fretwork with a quarter sheet of fine sandpaper while laying the piece on a flat surface. Then I sand the front with a shop-made sanding block, moving up progressively through the grits from 220 to 400. Finish sanding with a quarter sheet of 400- to 500-grit sandpaper to remove stubborn burrs and refine any problem areas a final time. Clean off dust with a soft tack cloth and use a clean, soft paintbrush to reach any dust left in tight areas.

Apply a finish of your choice; I used a natural non-toxic oil. To add extra luster, I let the piece dry completely, and then applied a coat of carnauba wax with a buffing wheel on a drill press. If you are going to use the piece as a hanging sign, run fine fishing line or string through the hole in the letter "E" and tie a 3" to 4" (7.6cm to 10.2cm) loop. *Note: If you want to use the sign as an applique, glue the piece to your backing board of choice before applying finishing oil and wax, because the finishing products will prevent the glue from adhering correctly.*

Patterns for the *Merry Christmas Signs* are in the pullout section.

Materials & Tools

Materials
- Wood, such as maple, cherry, or oak, ¾" (1.9cm) thick: sign with snowflake, 3½" x 9¼ (9cm x 23.5cm)
- Wood, such as maple, cherry, oak, ¾" 1.9cm) thick: plain sign, 3¼" x 6½ (8.53m x 16.5cm)
- Tape: clear packaging
- Spray adhesive: repositionable
- Pen or pencil
- Tack cloth
- Wood glue
- Sandpaper: assorted grits to 500
- Finish, natural oil, such as Circa 1850® Tera Nova NaturOil
- Finishing wax, such as carnauba (optional)
- Hanging string (optional)

Tools
- Scroll saw with blades: #1, #3 reverse-tooth
- Drill with bits: assorted
- Buffing wheel, such as Beall Buffing System (optional)
- Clean, soft paintbrush

The author used these products for the project. Substitute your choice of brands, tools, and materials as desired.

Wayne Fowler has been scrolling for over 30 years, first puzzles and then fretwork. Jacob Fowler has been drawing scroll saw designs since he was five (he drew a whale bank for his father, who collects whales). He got serious in his teens and has drawn well over a thousand designs since then. Together, Jacob and Wayne have published over 160 magazine articles, as well as the Woodworker's Pattern Book, available at Fox Chapel Publishing. They live in wood-rich Ontario, Canada, just outside Toronto. Find more of their work on Etsy at FantasiesISaw.

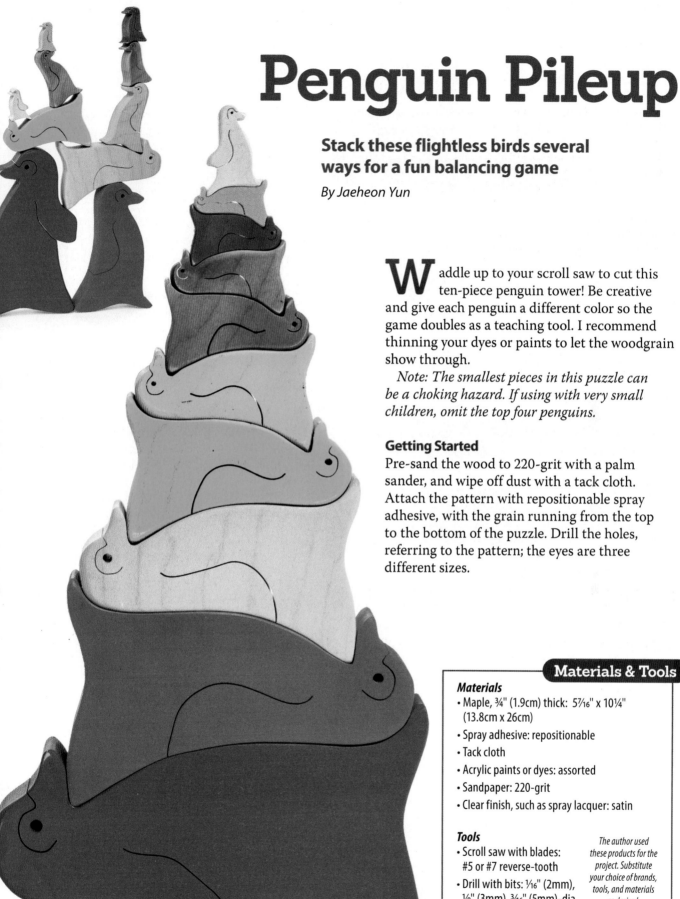

Penguin Pileup

Stack these flightless birds several ways for a fun balancing game

By Jaeheon Yun

Waddle up to your scroll saw to cut this ten-piece penguin tower! Be creative and give each penguin a different color so the game doubles as a teaching tool. I recommend thinning your dyes or paints to let the woodgrain show through.

Note: The smallest pieces in this puzzle can be a choking hazard. If using with very small children, omit the top four penguins.

Getting Started

Pre-sand the wood to 220-grit with a palm sander, and wipe off dust with a tack cloth. Attach the pattern with repositionable spray adhesive, with the grain running from the top to the bottom of the puzzle. Drill the holes, referring to the pattern; the eyes are three different sizes.

Materials & Tools

Materials
- Maple, ¾" (1.9cm) thick: 5⁷⁄₁₆" x 10¼" (13.8cm x 26cm)
- Spray adhesive: repositionable
- Tack cloth
- Acrylic paints or dyes: assorted
- Sandpaper: 220-grit
- Clear finish, such as spray lacquer: satin

Tools
- Scroll saw with blades: #5 or #7 reverse-tooth
- Drill with bits: ¹⁄₁₆" (2mm), ⅛" (3mm), ³⁄₁₆" (5mm)-dia.
- Sander: palm
- Paintbrushes

The author used these products for the project. Substitute your choice of brands, tools, and materials as desired.

Cutting and Finishing

Cut the puzzle on a scroll saw, starting with the perimeters of the pieces and finishing with the kerf details (i.e. the wings). Remove the patterns and sand away any fuzzies with 220-grit sandpaper. Soften the edges of the pieces, if desired. Wipe off dust once more with the tack cloth. Then apply your choice of paints or dyes; I used rainbow colors. Once dry, distress the edges slightly with sandpaper to give the pieces a folk-art feel. Finish with satin spray lacquer.

TIPS

DESIGN MODIFICATIONS

- *For greater stability, drill the eye holes lightly into the surface of each side, rather than drilling all the way through.*
- *Make it a number game by woodburning a number onto the belly of each penguin!*

Jaeheon Yun is a puzzle designer based in South Korea. He graduated from Seowon University with a degree in Industrial Design in 2004; then, just before his first child was born in 2011, be bought a scroll saw and began making toys. Find more of his work on Etsy at Namunolie.

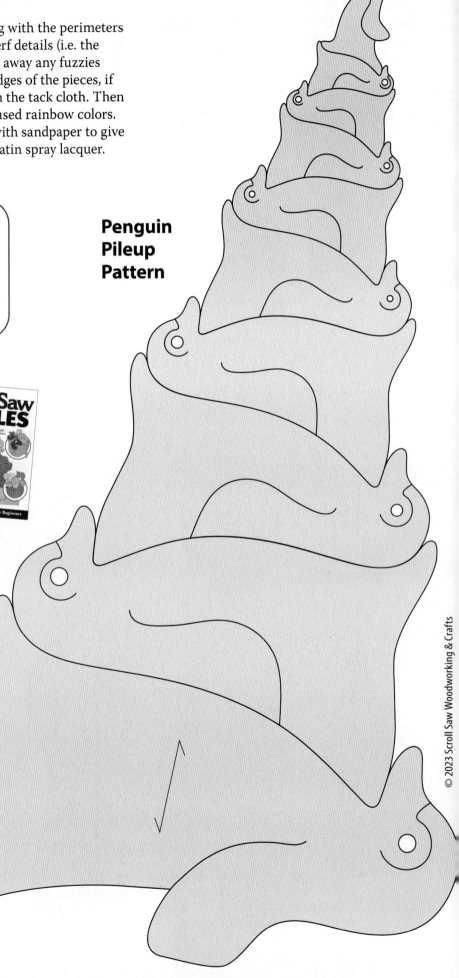

Penguin Pileup Pattern

Dangle Critter
ORNAMENTS

This project combines simple shapes with beginner compound-cutting techniques

By Sue Mey
Cut by Robert Carpentier

These dangle-legged critters are a cute addition to your holiday décor. Set them on a shelf, in potted plants, or any place where the legs can hang down. To hang them on a Christmas tree, simply thread string through the top opening. Alternately, you can set them among the tree branches with their legs hanging down. The critters' bodies are cut in the usual way on a scroll saw, but the shoes are compound-cut.

Getting Started

Photocopy each critter pattern and make six copies of the shoe patterns. Begin by preparing the blanks for the bodies. Apply masking tape or painter's tape to the blanks, and then attach the body patterns to the wood with spray adhesive or a glue stick. Then prepare the shoe blanks. For each shoe, apply masking tape or painter's tape to the wood. Fold the pattern on the centerline. Apply adhesive to the back of the pattern. Align the fold with the corner of the blank, and then press the pattern into place, removing all air bubbles.

Drilling and Cutting

For the body pieces, drill blade entry holes using the smaller drill bit and make the inside cuts using a #5 blade. Then cut the perimeter line. Secure the piece in a vise and drill two ¼" (6mm)-dia. holes approximately ½" (1.3cm) deep at the base of the body.

Cut the shoes, using a #7 blade to scroll the perimeter line on one side. When finished cutting, hold the blank together and wrap clear tape around the entire piece to secure it. Rotate the blank and cut the perimeter on the second side. Remove the tape and the waste wood to reveal a shoe. Drill a ¼" (6mm) hole, ⁵⁄₁₆" (8mm) deep, in the center of the top of each shoe.

Sanding and Finishing

Sand all pieces by hand to achieve a smooth finish. Begin with 120-grit sandpaper and work progressively to 320. If you wish to give the critters' bodies a cute and chunky appearance, I recommend softening the edges. Remove all the sanding dust with a stiff-bristled paintbrush.

The ornaments can be simply finished with wood stain for a uniform look or painted in festive colors with acrylic paint. After staining or painting, apply several thin coats of clear spray varnish to the bodies and shoes, allowing each coat to dry before applying the next.

When all pieces are completely dry, attach the legs. Wrap a ¼" (6mm)-wide strip of masking tape around the ends of each piece of cord to prevent fraying. Squeeze some cyanoacrylate (CA) glue into the hole at the base of the body. Twist the cord into the hole and allow the glue to dry. Repeat with all legs. Glue the cord into the holes in the shoes in the same way. Prior to gluing the shoes, make sure the cord is straight and the shoes face forward.

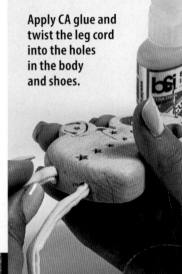

Apply CA glue and twist the leg cord into the holes in the body and shoes.

Materials & Tools

Materials
- Wood, such as pine, ⅝" (1.6cm) thick: body, 3⁹⁄₁₆" x 4¹³⁄₁₆" (9.1cm x 12.2cm)
- Wood, such as pine, 1³⁄₁₆" (3cm) square: 2 each shoes, 1⁹⁄₁₆" (4cm) long
- Cord: ¼" (6mm) thick: 2 each legs, 4" (10.2cm) long
- Tape: masking or painter's, clear packing
- Spray adhesive or glue stick
- Sandpaper: assorted grits to 320
- Glue: cyanoacrylate (CA)
- Wood stain (optional)
- Acrylic paints (optional)
- Finish, such as clear satin spray varnish

Tools
- Scroll saw with blades: #5 and #7 reverse-tooth
- Drill press with bits: ¹⁄₁₆" (2mm), ¼" (6mm)-dia.
- Vise
- Paintbrush: stiff-bristled
- Scissors

The author used these products for the project. Substitute your choice of brands, tools, and materials as desired.

Dangle Critter Ornaments Patterns

Sue Mey lives in Pretoria, South Africa. To see more of her work, including a wide variety of patterns and pattern-making tutorials available for purchase, visit scrollsawartist.com. She can be contacted at suem@storage.co.za. Her pattern book, Lighted Scroll Saw Projects, *is available from schifferbooks.com and other outlets.*

Robert Carpentier is a retired music teacher living in West Islip, N.Y. He began scrolling in 2010 and joined a local woodworking club. He studied intarsia with Judy Gale Roberts in 2012 and has since done many solo exhibits, displaying over 60 pieces in fretwork, intarsia, inlay, and segmentation. Reach out to Robert via email at rcarpen51@yahoo.com.

Piggy Bank

Easy to cut and construct, this functional project is a perfect way to introduce kids to the workshop

By Leonard Pick

SCROLLSAW
woodworking & CRAFTS

Winter 2023 - Issue 93

903 Square Street
Mount Joy, PA 17552

All patterns to be copied at 100% unless otherwise indicated.

Horizontal Advent Calendar	17	Fretwork Candy Ornaments	55
Bear Lookout	27	Happy Hanukkah!	57
Merry Christmas Sign	29	Poinsettia Box	61
Piggy Bank	36	Tiniest Cabin Construction Set	70
Santa and Sleigh Balance Toy	39	Layered Snowflake Ornaments	72
Intarsia Sports Car	51	Holiday Ornaments	***Web Extra!***

tterns

rs can
, making
e image.
de
the
original

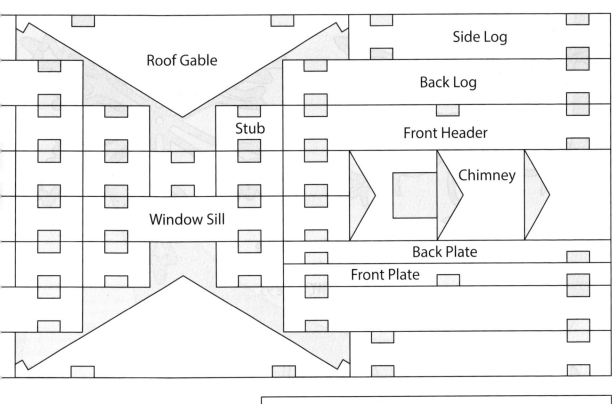

Roof Gable

Side Log

Back Log

Stub

Front Header

Chimney

Window Sill

Back Plate

Front Plate

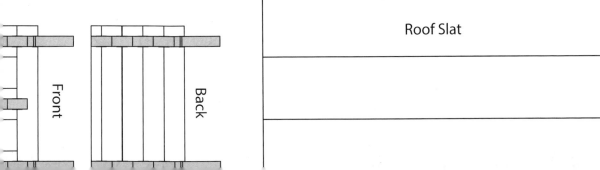

Front

Back

Roof Slat

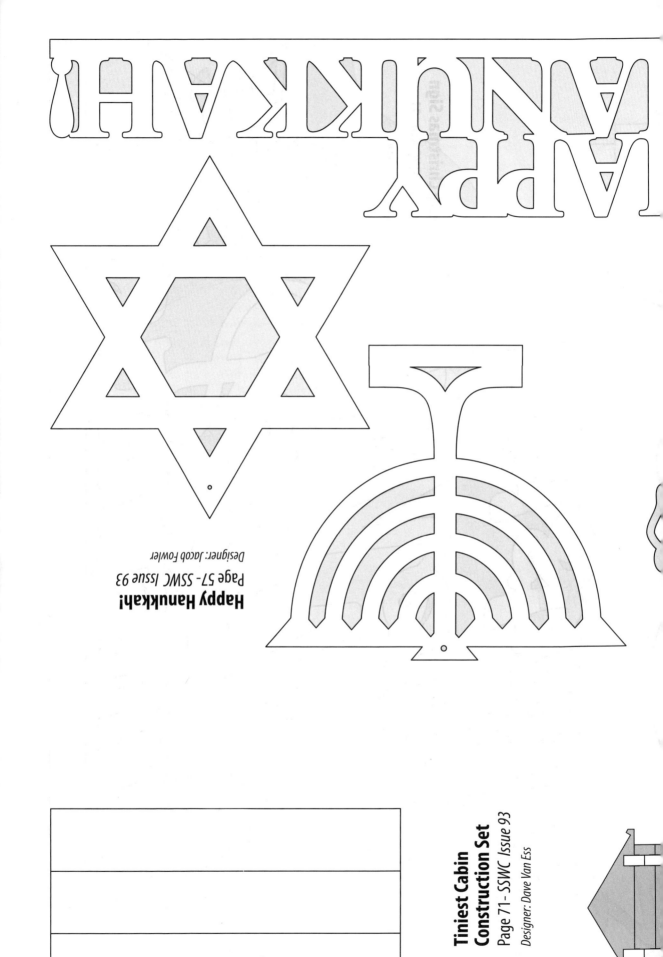

Happy Hanukkah!
Page 57 - SSWC Issue 93
Designer: Jacob Fowler

**Tiniest Cabin
Construction Set**
Page 71- SSWC Issue 93
Designer: Dave Van Ess

HAPPY ANUKKAH

A piggy bank is a great gift and easy to make. Kids love to watch their money add up. This one has clear sides so they can see their nest egg growing!

Getting Started

Photocopy the patterns. Choose your wood varieties; I like to use contrasting colors for the different layers. A nice hardwood for the centerpiece, part C, gives good strength to the finished item. Apply the patterns to their respective blanks with repositionable spray adhesive. Drill the entry hole for the center using a ¼" (6mm)-dia. bit. Then apply the patterns to the acrylic sides.

Cutting and Assembling

Cut the pieces, starting with the interiors and then ending with the perimeters. Cut the acrylic pieces, as well. Glue one of the Part B pieces to Part C. Clamp and let dry. After the glue has set, use a spindle sander to match the inner and outer body shapes. Then glue and clamp the other Part B piece to the opposite side of Part C and let dry. Sand the interior and exterior so the edges are flush. Add the Part A pieces to the outside of the pig in the same manner. Once dry, use the spindle sander to curve the sides of the head in gently and taper the face. Sand the entire surface of the project to 220-grit to smooth and soften the edges.

Cut the coin slot in the top of the bank. Secure the piece in a vise. With the ¼" (6mm)-dia. drill bit, drill two holes 1¼" (3.2cm) apart. Then drill additional holes in between to open the slot shape. Smooth the sides of the slot using files or a rotary tool with a 120-grit sanding drum.

Finishing

Finish with a few light coats of spray lacquer. When dry, place the acrylic pieces on each side of the body, mark the screw locations, and then drill the ½" (13mm) screws in place to attach the acrylic. Glue on the googly eyes. *Note: Add the acrylic after applying finish.*

Leonard Pick lives in west Milton, Pa., and began scrolling in 2005. Now retired and enjoying life with craft work, he also enjoys pyrography, glass etching, and airbrushing. Married 36 years, Leonard has one son, three stepsons, and many grandchildren. He is a member of several scroll saw groups on Facebook.

Materials & Tools

Materials

- Wood, such as pine or maple, ¾" (1.9cm) thick: part A, 2 each 7" x 9½" (17.8cm x 24.1cm)
- Wood, such as walnut or cherry, ¾" (1.9cm) thick: part B, 2 each 6" x 9½" (15.2cm x 24.1cm); part C, 6¼" x 9½" (15.9cm x 24.1cm)
- Clear acrylic, ⅛" (3mm) thick: sides, 2 each 6" x 7¾" (15.2cm x 19.7cm)
- Brass round-head screws: 16 each ½" (13mm) #6
- Spray adhesive: repositionable
- Wood glue
- Googly eyes: 2 each
- Sandpaper: assorted grits to 220
- Tack cloth
- Clear finish, such as spray lacquer: matte

Tools

- Scroll saw with blades: #5 to #7 reverse-tooth
- Drill with bit: ¼" (6mm)-dia.
- Rotary tool with sanding drum: 120-grit
- Files (optional)
- Sanders: oscillating drum with 100-grit; spindle
- Screwdriver
- Clamps
- Vise

The author used these products for the project. Substitute your choice of brands, tools, and materials as desired.

Piggy Bank Pattern

Additional patterns for the **PIGGY BANK** are in the pullout section.

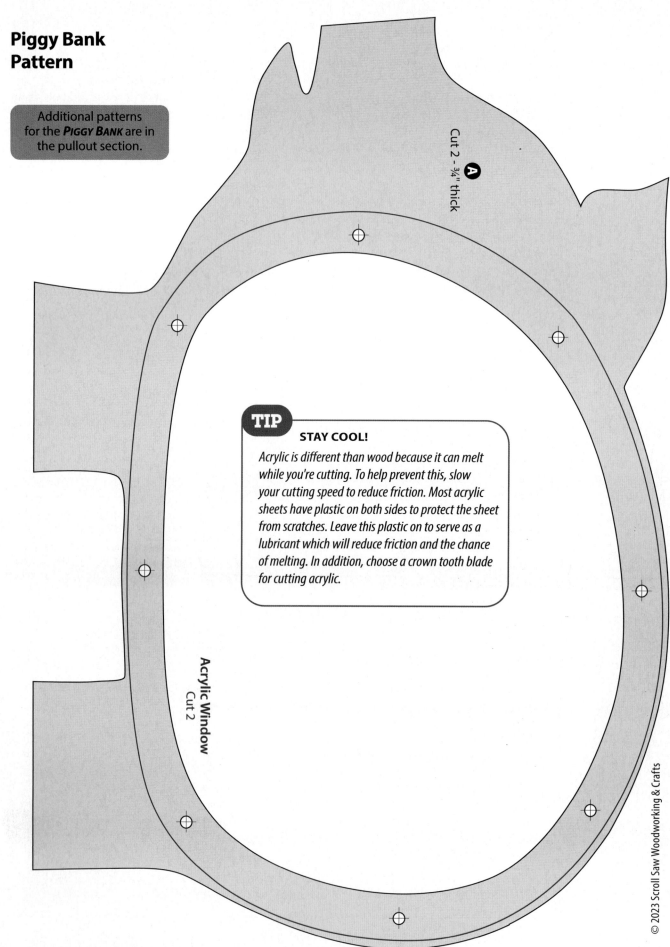

Cut 2 - ¾" thick

(A)

TIP

STAY COOL!

Acrylic is different than wood because it can melt while you're cutting. To help prevent this, slow your cutting speed to reduce friction. Most acrylic sheets have plastic on both sides to protect the sheet from scratches. Leave this plastic on to serve as a lubricant which will reduce friction and the chance of melting. In addition, choose a crown tooth blade for cutting acrylic.

Acrylic Window
Cut 2

© 2023 Scroll Saw Woodworking & Crafts

Santa and Sleigh Balance Toy

A sleepy village and a snowman counterweight complete this charming Christmas Eve tableau

By Richard Packer
Cut by Rolf Beuttenmuller

You can take many different approaches to this Christmas Eve balance toy. In its simplest form, just make the Santa, sleigh, and reindeer as a decorative ornament to hang on the tree or place on a mantle. Features like the background, village buildings, trees, and horse-drawn carriage are also optional. Or, build the whole project for a fun, traditional balance toy that can be tipped to rock to and fro. The nature of this design allows the rocking motion to last for quite a long time. *Note: The project is relatively fragile and should not be handled by unsupervised children.*

The sleigh rests on the opposite side of the fulcrum from the counterweight.

How it Works

Balance toys (also known as sky hook toys) are simple in operation. The Santa and reindeer are all one assembly. The Santa and reindeer piece sits atop a mechanical assembly that includes part N, which holds two nails. The tips of the nails fit in two matching holes in part M below. Using two nails instead of one allows the device to rock back and forth without twisting. Balance arc Q is attached to part N and the sleigh assembly. The arc supports the snowman counterweight below. This allows the whole assembly to swing back and forth on the dowel pedestal. Santa's waving arm, two bells, and two lanterns are attached with slightly protruding nails and swing with the sleigh's movement.

Successful operation will depend on a few factors, including the type (weight) of wood used, the balance point (fulcrum) where piece P is attached under the sleigh's tongue, the length of the tips of nails that extend out the bottom of part N, and the length and weight of the snowman counterweight.

The swinging assembly, including arc Q and the snowman, should all line up so the assembly swings straight between the L dowels. When at rest, the Santa and reindeer assembly should not hang down too far at either end.

Prepping and Cutting

Prepare wood to the thickness indicated on the pattern. Apply a spray adhesive, like Scotch 45, to the back of each pattern copy. Then attach the patterns to the stock and drill the blade-entry holes. *Note: Grain direction is critical for the sleigh-and-tongue piece; the grain should run along the length of the tongue.* Keep in mind that there are four styles of reindeer; you'll cut out two of each. Stack-cut the reindeer if desired. Cut the pieces on a scroll saw and carefully remove the patterns.

Along the top of the sleigh tongue, mark two parallel lines, centered and ⁹⁄₁₆" (1.4cm) apart. Thin the tongue to the lines using a band saw, handsaw, or scroll saw. Cut a centered slot in the bottom of Santa's arm (refer to pattern

pullout) and glue in a nut or small BB to add weight to encourage the bottom of the arm to swing down. Flip the snowman onto its front and cut the notch for the washers on the scroll saw. Sand each assembly piece progressively to 320-grit to remove fuzzies and lightly soften the edges. If you prefer to paint the pieces prior to assembly, do so now, referring to the Paint Notes on page 44. The test-cutter painted everything prior to assembly, except the top of part P and the underside of part A (for a wood-to-wood glue surface).

Assembling

1. Refer to the part's letters in the exploded view on page 42 during construction. Glue the runners to the sleigh, referring to the exploded drawings for placement. Glue the reindeer to both sides of the sleigh all along the tongue piece. *Note: You can*

The weighted snowman provides counterbalance to the sleigh.

Alternate Snowman Counterweight Patterns

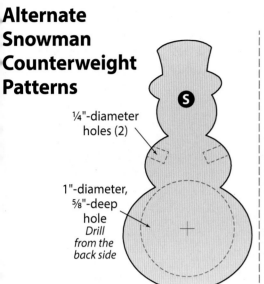

¼"-diameter holes (2)

1"-diameter, ⅝"-deep hole
Drill from the back side

Ⓢ

Fill hole with lead BBs.

Cut hole cover from thin wood or veneer.

arrange the reindeer in a number of ways based on your preference.

2. Glue Santa in place, in the center of the sleigh interior. Then attach the swinging arm, bells, and lanterns, by drilling the holes and installing a nail through each, keeping it loose enough that they sway easily. If needed, glue weights from washers or nuts at the bottom (back side) of each bell and lantern to improve their movement when the sleigh is swinging.

3. Cut the L dowels to size, and drill holes in part M and base K as shown in the patterns. Ensure that the holes are spaced equally. Install the dowels in the base, and then part M on top of the L dowels, with glue.

4. Build the rocking mechanism. The top of counterweight arc Q fits in a slot in part N. Drill N accurately, install the nails, and then glue this part to P. The tips of those nails must extend out of the bottom of part N equally. They will sit in the holes on top of part M. Watch that the nail spacing in N and hole spacing in M are identical. The hole's depth should be drilled the same amount so the whole sleigh/

reindeer assembly will sit and rock evenly.

5. Make the snowman counterweight. Glue nine washers in the cutout notch on the snowman's backside. Once dry, install the snowman at the bottom of counterweight arc Q with a screw. *Note: Alternatively, you could drill a hole in the back of the snowman, fill it with lead shot, and seal the BBs in with putty (see pattern above).*

6. Add the back panel. Photocopy the provided moon pattern and cut an identical circle of clear acrylic to place over it. Secure the moon and acrylic in place. (For more on the moon housing and lighting hardware, see Full Moon sidebar at right.) Glue and clamp back panel Y onto the back of the base.

Full Moon

If desired, cut out the moon image above and glue it to the face of back panel Y after painting the back. For more of a mystical effect, you could add a light. If adding a light, cut out a round hole as shown in the pattern. It should be precisely the same size as the moon image copy. Cut out a round piece of clear acrylic plastic ⅛" (3mm) thick or the thickness of back panel Y. Attach the paper moon copy to the acrylic disc with a light coat of spray adhesive. Fit the moon and disc in the hole from the back so the moon is flush with the face of back panel Y. Cut a slightly larger acrylic disc and glue it to the back of the moon. Then secure to the back of back panel Y. Add a light behind the moon. Use a table lamp, LED flashlight, night light, or a custom light attached to the back of the panel behind the moon.

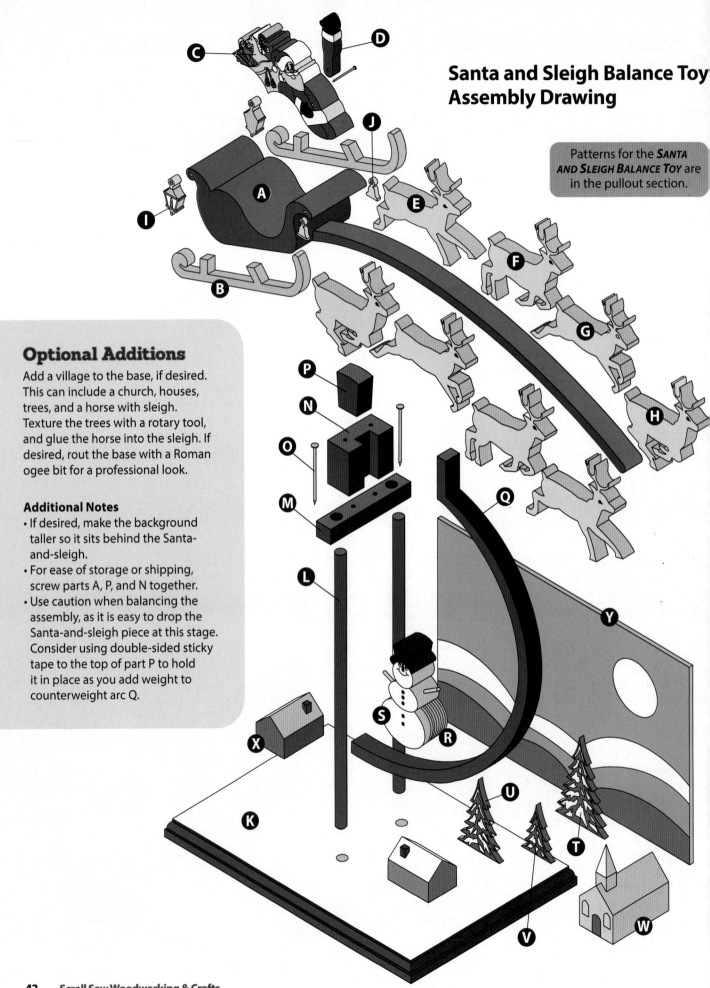

Santa and Sleigh Balance Toy Assembly Drawing

Patterns for the *SANTA AND SLEIGH BALANCE TOY* are in the pullout section.

Optional Additions

Add a village to the base, if desired. This can include a church, houses, trees, and a horse with sleigh. Texture the trees with a rotary tool, and glue the horse into the sleigh. If desired, rout the base with a Roman ogee bit for a professional look.

Additional Notes

• If desired, make the background taller so it sits behind the Santa-and-sleigh.

• For ease of storage or shipping, screw parts A, P, and N together.

• Use caution when balancing the assembly, as it is easy to drop the Santa-and-sleigh piece at this stage. Consider using double-sided sticky tape to the top of part P to hold it in place as you add weight to counterweight arc Q.

Parts List

	Part name	Quantity	Material	Dimensions	Presentation
A	Sleigh/Tongue	1	Maple, 2" (5.1cm) thick	1¾" x 13½" (4.5cm x 34.3cm)	Pattern
B	Sleigh Runner	2	Maple, ½" (1.3cm) thick	¾" x 4¼" (1.9cm x 10.8cm)	Pattern
C	Santa	1	Maple, ¾" (1.9cm) thick	2½" x 3" (6.4cm x 7.6cm)	Pattern
D	Santa's Arm	1	Maple, ½" (1.3cm) thick	⅜" x 1½" (1cm x 3.8cm)	Pattern
E	Deer	2	Maple, ⅜" (1cm) thick	2½" x 2⅔" (6.4cm x 7cm)	Pattern
F	Deer	2	Maple, ⅜" (1cm) thick	2¼" x 2⅝" (5.7cm x 6.7cm)	Pattern
G	Deer	2	Maple, ⅜" (1cm) thick	2½" x 2⅞" (6.4cm x 7.3cm)	Pattern
H	Deer	2	Maple, ⅜" (1cm) thick	2¾" x 3" (7cm x 7.6cm)	Pattern
I	Lantern	2	Maple, ⅜" (1cm) thick	½" x 1" (1.3cm x 2.5cm)	Pattern
J	Bell	2	Maple, ¼" (6mm) thick	⅝" x ⅞" (1.6cm x 2.2cm)	Pattern
K	Base	1	Baltic birch plywood, ⅜" (1cm) thick	8¼" x 12¼" (21cm x 31.1cm)	Dimensions
L	Support Leg	2	Dowel, ⁷⁄₁₆" (11mm) dia.	10½" (26.7cm) long	Dimensions
M	Support Crossbeam	1	Baltic birch plywood, ½" (1.3cm) thick	¾" x 3½" (1.9cm x 8.9cm)	Pattern
N	Fulcrum Base	1	Baltic birch plywood, ¾" (1.9cm) thick	1¼" x 1½" (3.2cm x 3.8cm)	Pattern
O	Nail	2	1¾" (4.4cm) long	N/A	N/A
P	Fulcrum Top	1	Baltic birch plywood, ¾" (1.9cm) thick	⅝" x 1" (1.6cm x 2.5cm)	Pattern
Q	Counterweight Arc	1	Baltic birch plywood, ½" (1.3) thick	8¾" (22.2cm) long	Pattern
R	Washer (optional)	9	1¼" (32mm) Fender washers	N/A	N/A
S	Snowman	1	Baltic birch plywood, ¾" (1.9cm) thick	1½" x 2⅝" (3.8cm x 6.7cm)	Pattern
T	Largest Tree	1	Baltic birch plywood, ¼" (6mm) thick	1¾" x 2⅞" (4.4cm x 7.3cm)	Pattern
U	Middle Tree	1	Baltic birch plywood, ¼" (6mm) thick	1½" x 2⅜" (3.8cm x 6cm)	Pattern
V	Smallest Tree	1	Baltic birch plywood, ¼" (6mm) thick	1⅛" x 1½" (2.9cm x 3.8cm)	Pattern
W	Church	1	Baltic birch plywood, 1½" (3.8cm) thick	2½" x 3" (6.4cm x 7.6cm)	Pattern
X	House	1	Baltic birch plywood, 1½" (3.8cm)	1¾" x 2" (4.4cm x 5.1cm)	Pattern
Y	Scenic Background	1	Baltic birch plywood, ¼" (6mm)	9" x 11¾" (22.8cm x 29.8cm)	Dimensions

Materials & Tools

Materials
- Maple, assorted thickness and dimensions (see Parts List)
- Baltic birch plywood, assorted thickness and dimensions (see Parts List)
- Oak dowels, ⁷⁄₁₆" (11mm)-dia.: Part L, 2 each 10½" (26.7cm) long
- Wire nails: 2 each #16, 1½" (3.8cm) long; 4 each #9, ½" (1.3cm) long
- Washers: 9 each 1¼" (3.2cm) fender
- Lead BBs (optional)

- Graphite paper (optional)
- Pencil
- Wood glue
- Dowels
- Clear acrylic plastic, ⅛" (3mm) thick: 2 each approx. 3" (7.6cm) square
- LED flashlight or night light (optional)
- Acrylic paints: assorted (see Paint Notes on page 44)
- Spray adhesive, such as Scotch 4S

- Sandpaper: assorted up to 320-grit
- Clear finish, such as spray lacquer: matte or semigloss

Tools
- Scroll saw with blades: #3 to #9 reverse tooth
- Saws: band or hand (optional)
- Drill press with bits: ¹⁄₁₆" (2mm), ¼" (6mm) ⁷⁄₁₆" (11mm)-dia.
- Router with Roman ogee bit: ⁵⁄₃₂" (4mm)-dia. (optional)

- Rotary tool (optional)
- Sander
- Paintbrushes
- Toothpicks
- Clamps

The author used these products for the project. Substitute your choice of brands, tools, and materials as desired.

Paint Notes

Background
Sky: English navy (4)

Snowflakes: white (3)

Mountain top layer: white (3)

Mountain middle layer: 4 parts white (3), 1 part English navy (4)

Mountain bottom layer: 1 part white (3), 1 part English navy (4)

Base: 4 parts white (3), 1 part English navy (4)

Santa and Sleigh Assembly
Reindeer: bright green (1), medium yellow (1), coffee latte (2), lipstick red (1)

Sleigh and tongue: lipstick red (1)

Sleigh runners: silver metallic (3)

Bells: lipstick red (1), medium yellow (1), gold metallic (3)

Lanterns: hunter green (1), white (3), gold metallic (3), cobalt (1)

Santa: lipstick red (1), peach (3), white (3), pure black (4)

Optional Extras
Trees: hunter green (1)

Snow accents on trees and roofs: 4 parts white (3), 1 part English navy (4)

Buildings: cobalt blue (1), English navy (4), fawn (2), hunter green (1), lipstick red (1)

Windows: medium yellow (1)

1 FolkArt®
2 Americana®
3 Craftsmart®
4 Apple Barrel®

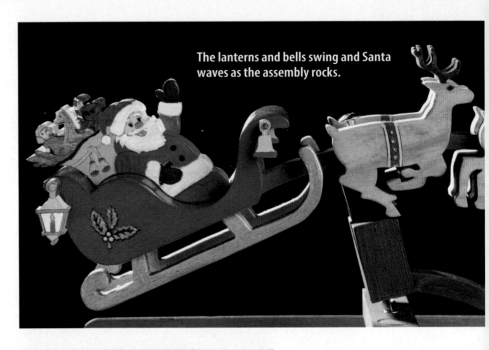

The lanterns and bells swing and Santa waves as the assembly rocks.

Painting and Finishing
If you have not yet painted the pieces, do so now, referring to the Paint Notes (at left). *Note: If desired, lightly burn the painting details onto the surface of the pieces with a laser; if you prefer not to freehand, you could also use graphite paper and a pencil.* When painting the background, you can use round-centered toothpicks cut in half, dipping the cut end in white paint and randomly dabbing it around the sky surface for a snowy effect. When dry, spray with several light coats of matte or semigloss lacquer.

Richard Packer began Forest Street Designs as a family business in 1971. He made unfinished wood products for many years before focusing on woodworking plans for toys, clocks, birdhouses, furniture, marble games, and more. Learn more at Richard's website, foreststreetdesigns.com.

Rolf Beuttenmuller started scrolling in 2004 after his wife, June, bought him a scroll saw for his birthday. He joined a local club and enjoys new and challenging projects. His motto is, "I don't know that I can't, therefore I can." Rolf retired from Brookhaven National Lab after 34 years of designing and building special devices for high energy and photon science research. He lives in Bellport, N.Y.

Mid-Century Modern ORNAMENTS

Elevate your tree décor with these classy, stylized baubles

By Frederick P. Arndt
Cut by Joe Pascucci

The mid-century modern period, spanning the 1940s through the 1960s, introduced the world to a new era of design with clean lines and geometric shapes that remains popular today. Using this aesthetic, I've created a number of simple wooden ornaments. They are a low-cost alternative to purchasing vintage bulbs from an antique store. Stack cut a bunch and you'll have a treeful in no time!

Getting Started
Photocopy the patterns and prepare the blanks by sanding them with 150- and then 220-grit sandpaper. Remove dust with a clean cloth. If you are stack-cutting, secure your blanks by wrapping the edges with clear packaging tape to hold them together. Attach the patterns to the blanks using scroller's tape; alternatively, you can cover the blanks with blue painter's tape and attach the patterns with repositionable spray adhesive. Drill the blade-entry holes for the frets and hanger.

Cutting and Sanding
Cut the fretwork, making the interior cuts first. Remove the patterns, and gently sand the surfaces with 220- and then 320-grit sandpaper. Remove dust with a tack cloth. Finish with clear gloss polyurethane or Danish oil to accentuate the beauty of the wood.

> **TIP**
> **HARDWOODS HELP**
> *I recommend using natural hardwoods for these ornaments, as they are strong and durable.*

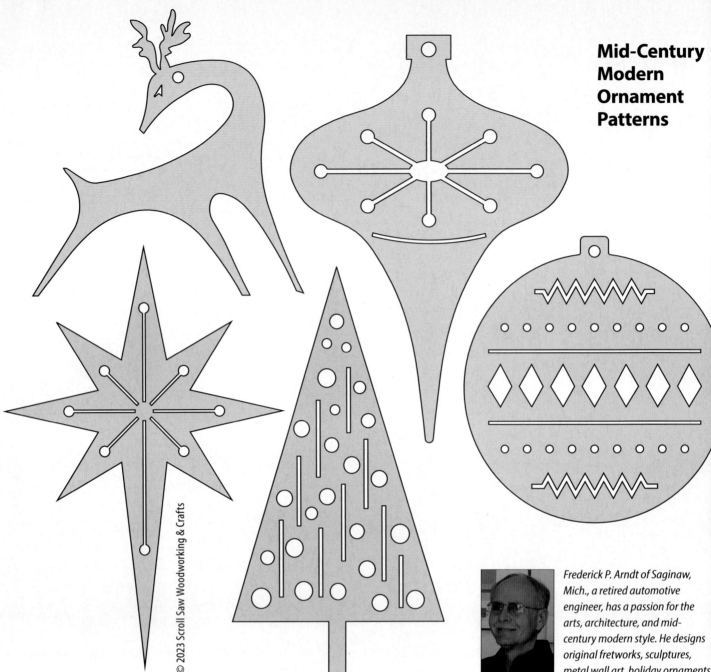

Mid-Century Modern Ornament Patterns

© 2023 Scroll Saw Woodworking & Crafts

Frederick P. Arndt of Saginaw, Mich., a retired automotive engineer, has a passion for the arts, architecture, and mid-century modern style. He designs original fretworks, sculptures, metal wall art, holiday ornaments, and kitchen accessories. His work can be found in galleries across the United States and online at his Fred Arndt Artworks Etsy Store. Contact Frederick at fparndt@aol.com.

Joe Pascucci started scrolling nearly 30 years ago. He also enjoys woodturning and other types of woodworking. Joe is a retired police sergeant and construction superintendent, and is the founding president of the Long Island Scroll Saw Association. When Joe's not in the woodshop, he can be found gardening, traveling, and spending time with his grandkids. To see more of Joe's work, visit the Members section of liwoodworkers.org.

Materials & Tools

Materials
- Wood, such as walnut, ⁵⁄₁₆" (8mm) thick: teardrop and tree, 3" x 4¼" (7.6cm x 10.8cm)
- Wood, such as walnut, ⁵⁄₁₆" (8mm) thick: ball, 3" (7.6cm) square
- Wood, such as cherry, ⁵⁄₁₆" (8mm) thick: deer, 2⅞" x 3" (7.3cm x 7.6cm)
- Wood, such as walnut, ⁵⁄₁₆" (8mm) thick: star, 3" x 4" (7.6cm x 10.2cm)
- Tape: blue painter's, clear packaging (optional), scroller's (optional)
- Spray adhesive: repositionable
- Sandpaper: assorted grits to 320
- Tack cloth

- Finish, such as natural Danish oil or gloss polyurethane
- Decorative string

Tools
- Scroll saw with blades: #3 reverse-tooth
- Drill with bit: small

The author used these products for the project. Substitute your choice of brands, tools, and materials as desired.

Easy Hardwood Toolkit

Have fun making this educational toy for the little handyperson in your life

By Rita Cels

Children are constantly watching grown-ups, and by imitating them they learn about the world around them. I designed this toolkit to be a fun imaginative toy, and also a shape puzzle! Teach your little ones hand-eye coordination and spatial recognition as they fit the tools into their respective spots. It's both educational and fun. Play around with different hardwoods for different looks. For added durability, make the box from a hardwood, like maple. You are only limited by your imagination!

Getting started
Make three copies of the patterns. Attach two copies to the box blanks with repositionable spray adhesive. From the third copy, separate the tool patterns, then attach each to a hardwood of your choice.

1 Prepare the box. With a #5 reverse-tooth blade, cut one box outline, excluding the handle. Remove the pattern and set this piece aside. Cut another box perimeter that includes the handle. On this piece, drill a ¹⁄₁₆" (2mm)-dia. entry hole in each tool space.

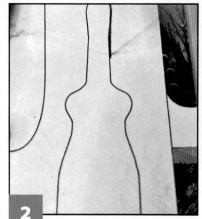
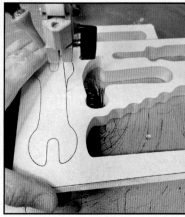

2 Cut the tools out. Cut along the outside edge of the tool shapes on the pattern. This will allow more space for the tools to fit into their respective wells later. If you are making all the tools from pine, the waste portions in this step will be your tools. If you're using different hardwoods to make the tools, set the waste pieces aside.

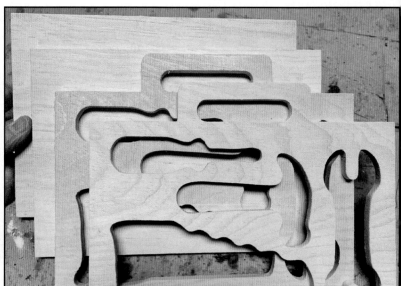

3 Cut all pieces of the box. Using a band saw, rip each piece of the box into two ³⁄₈" (1cm)-thick slices. You will end up with two outside parts of the box and two inner portions where the tools will go. Sand the striations smooth, and make sure the recesses where the tools will rest are smooth.

No Band Saw?

If you don't have access to a band saw, make the kit from ³⁄₈" (1cm)-thick plywood on a scroll saw. Cut two pieces of the box with the handle and two pieces without the handle.

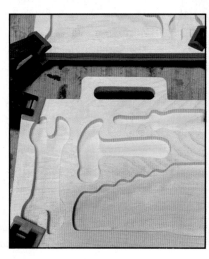

4 Glue the box. To make the box, glue each piece with a handle to a piece with no handle, matching the edges carefully. Clamp and let dry. The clamp the completed sides together, solid sides out, and sand the edges flush.

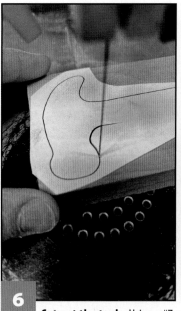

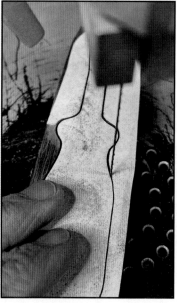

5 **Attach the hinges.** Clamp the two completed sides together, and then mark the screw holes for the hinges on the bottom of the kit. Drill ¹⁄₁₆" (2mm)-dia. pilot holes for the screws. Attach the hinges and set the box aside.

6 **Cut out the tools.** Using a #7 reverse-tooth blade, cut out each tool. Use the inside edge of the lines on the pattern to allow more space for the tools to fit into the box.

Sanding and Finishing

Sand any rough, sharp edges off the tools. *Note: If you chose to make pine tools from the box waste pieces, you will have to sand them thinner so they fit into the kit when it's closed.* Check to see if the tools fit into the box. If they catch anywhere, sand them until they can easily be taken in and out of their pockets. Coat the tools with a child-safe finish, such as a 4:1 mineral oil/beeswax mixture.

If you chose to make the whole kit out of pine, you can leave the tools natural or paint them bright colors with nontoxic acrylic paint. You can also add magnets with CA glue to help keep the box closed. *Note: If you're concerned that the magnet will fall out, secure the box closed with a hook-and-eye mechanism instead.*

Materials & Tools

Materials
- Wood, such pine, ¾" (1.9cm) thick: box, 2 each 7" x 18" (17.8cm x 45.7cm)
- Wood, such as walnut, ½" (1.3cm) thick: saw, 2¾" x 5½" (7cm x 14cm)
- Wood, such as padauk, ½" (1.3cm) thick: screwdriver, 1¼" x 4¼" (3.2cm x 10.8cm)
- Wood, such as yellowheart, ½" (1.3cm) thick: wrench, 1¾" x 4½" (4.4cm x 11.4cm)
- Wood, such as cherry, ½" (1.3cm) thick: hammer, 2¾" x 4" (7cm x 10.2cm)
- Wood, such as plywood, ¾" (1.9cm) thick: frame, 7" x 18" (17.8cm x 45.7cm) (optional)
- Spray adhesive: repositionable
- Sanding sponges: medium and fine
- Glue: cyanoacrylate (CA)
- Hinges: 2 each 1" (2.5cm)
- Finish, such as mineral oil or beeswax
- Nontoxic acrylic paints: blue, brown, red, silver (optional)
- Neodymium magnets, ¼" (6mm)-dia.: 2 each ⅛" (3mm) thick (optional)
- Hook-and-eye closure (opitonal)

Tools
- Scroll saw with blades: #5, #7 reverse-tooth
- Band saw
- Drill press with bits: ¹⁄₁₆" (2mm), ¼" (6mm)-dia.
- Router with roundover bit: ⅛" (3mm)-dia.
- Scissors
- Clamps

The author used these products for the project. Substitute your choice of brands, tools, and materials as desired.

Rita Cels is a retired teacher and self-taught scroller from Leduc, Alberta, Canada. Although much of Rita's time is spent making wooden children's toys, in her spare time, she loves designing special boxes using a variety of woods and techniques. Check out Rita Cels Creations on Instagram and Etsy.

Toy Toolkit
Pattern

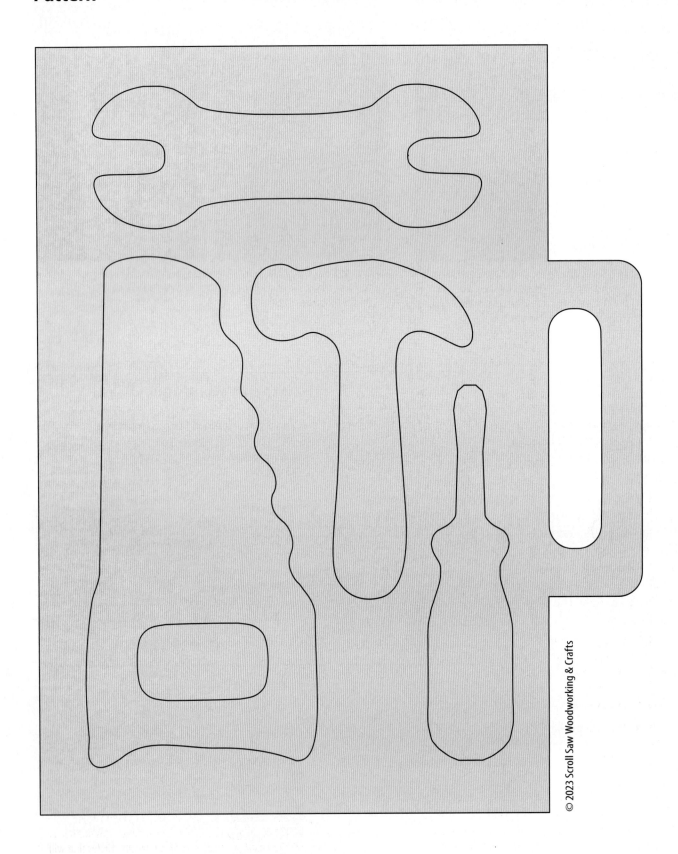

Intarsia Sports Car

Capture the feeling of a road rally with this spirited classic convertible

By Janette Square

I know very little about classic cars, but I do have a great appreciation for them. This design was inspired by an old photo of my dad's car I found from decades ago.

Getting Started

Prepare the pattern, select your woods, and apply the pattern pieces. You will need five copies of the pattern, plus a master copy. Cover the wood with clear packaging tape before coating with an adhesive spray and applying the pattern pieces.

1 **Drill the holes.** Drill the nine holes where pieces will be inserted: two in the outer grill piece, two in the red pieces for the fog lights, two in the gray rim of the fog lights for the light insert, one in each of the dark tire centers, and one in the gray area of the front tire. I suggest using a ⅛" (3mm)-dia. brad point bit. Place a scrap piece under the workpiece when drilling to avoid tear-out. Alternatively, set the drill press so just the point of the bit comes through the bottom of the piece, and then flip the piece over to complete the hole. This produces a clean hole.

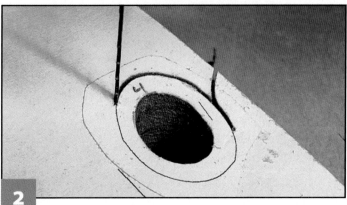

2 **Cut out all drilled pieces.** I use a #7 modified geometric blade, except for the seat sections, risers, and backer. Cut out the drilled areas before cutting the perimeter of the pieces. When cutting out the center of the lights, insert the blade into the hole, cut toward the edge, and then turn clockwise. Cut a short distance and back the blade out. Rotate the piece and feed the blade backwards into the kerf you just cut. Cut counterclockwise around the perimeter, following the line closely to complete the cut. Cut the infill pieces in the same manner. This method is optional, but I find it works best when cutting out smaller circles that will receive inlay pieces. Cut the perimeter of the car seat pieces. Then switch to a finer #3 blade to separate the individual pieces.

3 **Finish cutting and assemble.** Cut out remaining pieces and assemble the project on the master pattern. Make any minor fit adjustments, if needed.

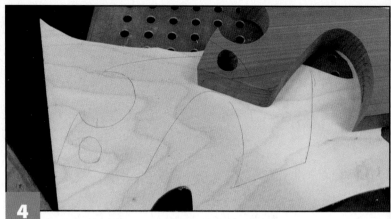

4 **Cut out the risers.** I use a #2 blade. Some areas may need risers, depending on the thickness of the wood you started with. The right front panel should be raised ⅛" (3mm) above the hood. Glue this riser into place. The chrome bumper, headlights, and front grill should all sit higher than the body parts. Don't attach these risers until shaping is done in case adjustments are needed.

5 **Shape the chassis.** Start by shaping the hood. The side where the hood meets the windshield should be slightly lower than the front. The entire piece is tapered downward toward the front and to the left toward the windshield. Slightly curve the sides where they meet the front quarter panels. Then shape the front quarter panel to the left of the hood. Draw a light line to indicate where it meets the hood. The right side should taper down to gradually disappear behind the hood piece. Keep the left side slightly higher than the hood and round it down to where they meet. Finally, shape the right front quarter panel and driver's door. These are best shaped together. Using double-sided tape, attach the pieces to a ¼" (6mm)-thick sanding shim. Be sure the riser for the quarter panel is glued on. It will sit ⅛" (3mm) higher than the driver's door. Sand the pieces together, tapering them lower toward the back of the car. The two pieces should blend smoothly where they meet. Round the front quarter panel to meet the hood. This piece should be higher than the hood by about ¼" (6mm) at the front. Shape the rocker panel below at the same angle, and then round over the bottom slightly.

Landmarks for Shaping

For shaping guidance, refer to the angle and side photos of the finished project on page 51. For the perspective aspect of the project, an easy rule to keep in mind is that everything to the right of the right headlight is tapered to the right, and everything to the left is tapered to the left.

6 **Shape the windshield and its frame.** Draw a pencil line along the windshield frame piece where it meets the hood. Taper this piece along the drawn line, leaving it about 1/16" (2mm) higher than the hood. The right side should be slightly lower than the side panel so it appears to disappear behind it. Angle the entire piece back slightly where it meets the windshield. Shape the bottom of the windshield to follow the contour of the lower frame piece from side to side. Overall, it should sit slightly lower than the frame. Taper the piece downward from bottom to top. The top will be lower and the top left side slightly lower still. Then shape the windshield frame. Taper the top and side windshield frame pieces to follow the contour of the windshield, leaving them slightly higher.

7 **Shape the tires.** The should taper slighty toward the right.

8 **Shape and add indents to the bumper.** Roughly shape the contour of the bumper to follow the line of the hood. Add risers as needed. The bumper should be higher than the front tire and the hood. With a sanding bit in a rotary tool, create two indents in each bumper piece.

9 **Smooth the bumpers.** Fine-tune and smooth with a rounded profile sander.

10 **Shape the seat.** Rough shape the back of the car seat first. Draw a line where the seat back pieces meet to use as a guide. It's easier to shape these small pieces if you make a sacrificial frame to contain them while shaping. This will ensure they are all uniform. Using a piece of pine or other soft scrap wood, cut out the shape of the seat with a #3 reverse-tooth or #3 MG blade and insert the seat pieces. Attach the seat pieces and the frame to a sanding shim with two-sided tape. Once the desired height and angle are achieved, remove the pieces and hand-sand each one individually. Each piece should be slightly rounded over to give the appearance of tufted leather.

11 **Shape all remaining pieces.** The grill pieces should follow the same contour of the hood. Rough-shape the three pieces together with a sanding shim, and then sand the two inner pieces slightly lower. The outer grill piece should sit slightly higher than the hood. The wheel well pieces are tapered down and to the left to add depth behind the tires. The back quarter panel beside the seat is rounded over to give it a bubble-like appearance, keeping the rim where it meets the wheel well sharp. It should sit just higher than the seat. The lights should sit just above their rims and are rounded down to meet the rim. The light and rims sit just higher than the car body. Reduce the thickness of the front tire on the left to sit below the valance under the bumper. The bumper guards should be higher than the bumper.

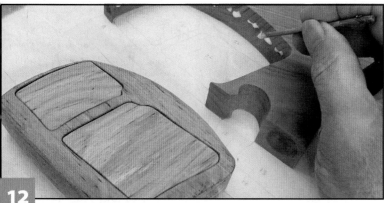

12 **Glue your project.** Glue the risers to their respective pieces. I glued smaller areas together in segments. I find it's easier to assemble this way when working with small pieces. Reassemble the entire project often to ensure everything still fits together well. I glued the tires, windshield, grill pieces, and seat assembly. Once these are dry, complete the gluing.

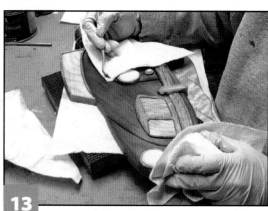

13 **Apply finish.** Use your finish of choice and be sure to wipe away any excess.

14 **Cut out the backer.** Trace the project onto the backer and cut it out; I use a #2 blade. Remember to apply black marker around the backer edges to make it less noticeable, if desired.

15 **Apply the backer and hanger.** Glue the backer to the project and clamp. Once dry, apply the hanger and enjoy!

Pattern for the **INTARSIA SPORTS CAR** is in the pullout section.

Janette Square is an internationally known intarsia artist and designer. She has been a regular contributor to Scroll Saw Woodworking and Crafts magazine for nearly 20 years. She specializes in realistic animals and custom pet portraits, but also designs and creates many other subjects as well. Living in the small village of Yachats (Ya-Hots) on the Oregon coast has been a great inspiration for many of her designs. Look for Janette's new book available now. It contains 11 brand-new designs at all skill levels. Detailed instructions and in-depth skill building challenges will guide you to becoming a better intarsia artist regardless of your skill level. You can contact Janette through her website, square-designs.com, or email her at janettesquare@gmail.com.

Fretwork Candy Ornaments

Nostalgic decorations are a sweet treat for your tree this year

By Keith Fenton
Cut by Joe Pascucci

These cute fretwork candies evoke memories of Christmases past. This is a great project to practice stack cutting, so you can make more than a dozen ornaments in no time. Hang them around the house, or attach them to wrapped packages to add an extra bonus gift to your presents.

Getting Started

Photocopy the patterns, sizing them up if desired for ease of cutting. Prepare the wood by sanding both sides with 100-grit sandpaper by itself or in a hand-held orbital sander to remove planer marks and smooth the wood. Graduate to 150-grit. Clean all the dust from the wood with a tack cloth.

Place a layer of blue painter's or masking tape over the entire surface of the wood to help prevent burning and for easy pattern removal. If you prefer to use packaging tape to prevent burning, you may find it easier to put the tape over the pattern rather than under it. Apply the pattern over the masking tape by lightly spraying the back with a light misting of repositionable spray adhesive. Allow the spray to tack up for a few seconds until it feels sticky like masking tape, and then apply the pattern to your wood pieces, smoothing out any bubbles. *Note: If you are stack cutting, use packaging tape all around the edges to attach additional layers of wood under your first layer.*

Use a small bit in your drill press to drill entry holes for the interior cuts. Use an appropriate-sized bit for the hanging holes. After drilling, turn the pieces over and sand the backs so that they lay perfectly flat while cutting.

> **TIP**
>
> #### DOUBLE UP
>
> *Stack cutting two layers at once makes intricate cutting easier. Thicker wood offers more resistance to the blade and makes small details easier to cut.*

Cutting and Finishing

Use a #2/0 reverse-tooth scroll saw blade to scroll the designs, starting with the interior cuts and then moving to the perimeters. If you are stack cutting, be sure that your layers don't separate as you cut the perimeter. You can always stop partway through the perimeter cut to add more tape.

After cutting, use sandpaper or an orbital sander to carefully remove burrs. You can start with 150-grit sandpaper and finish with 220-grit. Sand gently to avoid catching an edge in the delicate fretwork areas. Use a knife or sanding stick to remove any burrs that remain. When sanding is finished, clean all the dust from your wood with a soft cloth.

Spray with several light coats of a varnish of your choice, allowing ample drying time between coats. For a smoother finish, sand lightly by hand with 400- or 600-grit sandpaper, and then clean off the dust before applying a final coat. Allow the varnish to dry. Tie on a cord for hanging and enjoy!

Patterns for the *FRETWORK CANDY ORNAMENTS* are in the pullout section.

Materials & Tools

Materials
- Wood, such as cherry, maple, mahogany, walnut, or Baltic birch plywood, ⅛" to ¼" (3mm to 6mm) thick: sized for patterns
- Spray adhesive: repositionable spray
- Tape: blue painter's or masking, clear packaging (optional)
- Sandpaper: various grits to 600
- Clean cloth
- Finish, such as spray varnish
- Small cord or hanger

Tools
- Scroll saw with blades: #2/0 reverse-tooth
- Drill press with bit: small
- Sander: orbital with grits up to 220 (optional)
- Knife or sanding stick

The author used these products for the project. Substitute your choice of brands, tools, and materials as desired.

Keith Fenton has been designing scroll saw patterns for several years alongside his partner, Sheila Landry. Together they have contributed patterns and articles to several woodworking and painting magazines. Visit their web site at sheilalandrydesigns.com to see their entire selection of patterns (including free samples). If you have any questions about this project, you can reach Keith at sheilalandrydesigns@gmail.com.

Joe Pascucci started scrolling nearly 30 years ago. He also enjoys woodturning and other types of woodworking. Joe is a retired police sergeant and construction superintendent, and is the founding president of the Long Island Scroll Saw Association. When Joe's not in the woodshop, he can be found gardening, traveling, and spending time with his grandkids. To see more of Joe's work, visit the Members section of liwoodworkers.org.

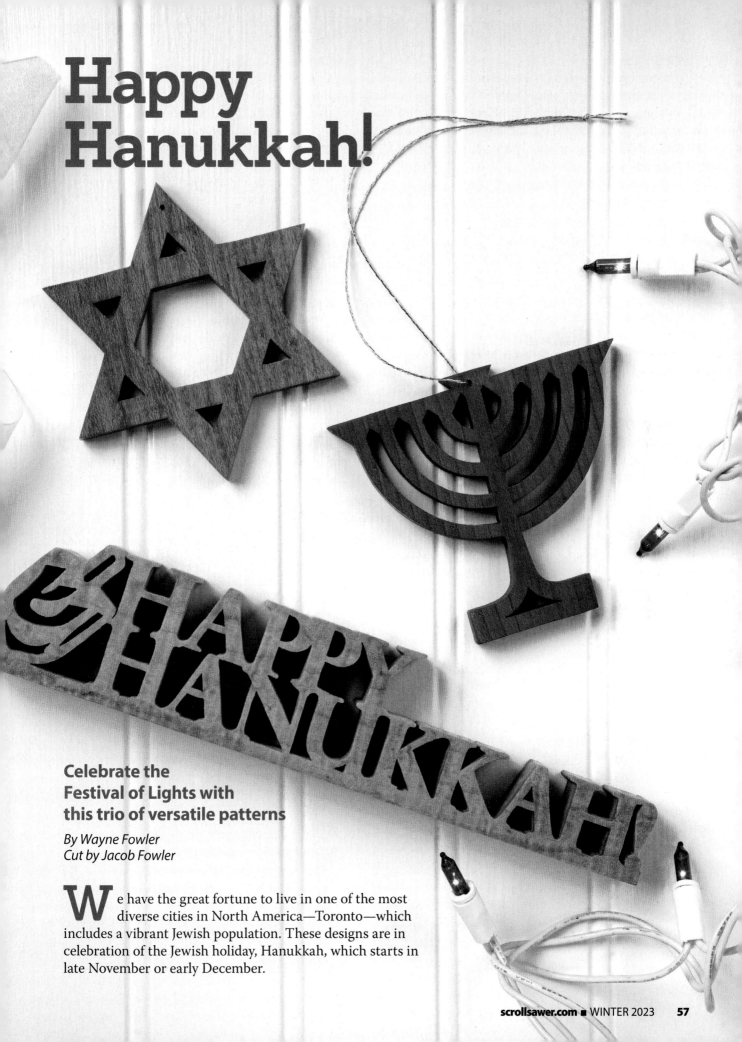

Happy Hanukkah!

Celebrate the Festival of Lights with this trio of versatile patterns

By Wayne Fowler
Cut by Jacob Fowler

We have the great fortune to live in one of the most diverse cities in North America—Toronto—which includes a vibrant Jewish population. These designs are in celebration of the Jewish holiday, Hanukkah, which starts in late November or early December.

Getting Started

Photocopy the pattern you wish to cut. The Star of David and menorah patterns work best as ornaments or appliqués with thinner wood (about ¼" [6mm] thick) that has a little character, like maple, oak, cherry, or similar. The "Happy Hanukkah!" is intended to be freestanding and should be cut from similar wood thick enough to stand on its own (¾" [1.9cm] or thicker).

Cover the wood with clear packaging tape, and then attach the pattern to the tape with spray adhesive. The clear tape lets you see the wood underneath so you can properly place the pattern; it also helps to lubricate the blade while you cut and allows for quicker pattern removal once you are done. *Note: If desired, stack-cut two pieces of thin hardwood for the star and menorah so you can cut multiples at once.*

Drill the blade-entry holes in the waste areas where the interior cuts will go. You can use a larger drill bit for the bigger space in the star, which will make it easier to feed the blade through. Some of the smaller holes (such as those in the lettering and dreidel) will require a smaller drill bit, however. Also drill a hole for string in the menorah and Star of David if planning to use them as ornaments.

Cutting

Cut the project on a scroll saw, starting with the interior cuts. The size of the blade you use depends on the wood thickness and density, as well as the level of detail in the cut. For most of these pieces, a #3 reverse-tooth blade will suffice, but for the smaller cuts, such as those in the dreidel, it may be better to use a #1 blade. Finally, cut the perimeter of the piece. Remove the patterns.

Sanding and Finishing

Sand the pieces; I usually hand-sand the back of the fretwork with a quarter sheet of fine sandpaper while resting it on another board. Then I sand the front with a shop-made sanding block, moving up progressively through the grits from 220 to 400. Wipe off dust with a tack cloth.

Give the piece a final sand with a sanding block. Then follow up with a quarter sheet of 400- to 500-grit sandpaper to remove stubborn burrs and refine any problem areas once more. Clean off dust with a clean, soft paintbrush. If you are using a disc or belt sander, sand the bottom of the lettered sign so that it sits level.

For any piece, apply a finish of your choice; I used a natural non-toxic oil. To add extra luster, I applied a coat of carnauba wax with a buffing wheel on a drill press once the oil dried. If you are going to use the Star of David and menorah as ornaments, run fine fishing line or string through the holes at the top and hang as desired. For appliques, glue the piece to a backing board of your choice before you apply finishing oil; then let the glue dry and apply the finish.

Patterns for **HAPPY HANUKKAH!** are in the pullout section.

Materials & Tools

Materials
- Wood, such as maple, cherry or oak, ¼" (6mm) thick: Star of David, approx. 3¾" (9.5cm) square; menorah, 3½" x 4" (8.9cm x 10.2cm)
- Wood, such as maple, cherry, or oak, ¾" (1.9cm) thick: lettering, 2" x 9" (5.1cm x 22.9cm)
- Tape: clear packaging
- Spray adhesive
- Pen or pencil
- Tack cloth
- Wood glue (optional)
- Sandpaper: assorted grits to 500

- Natural oil finish, such as Danish oil or Terra Nova NaturOil
- Finishing wax, such as carnauba (optional)
- Fishing line, string, or ribbon

Tools
- Scroll saw with blades: #1, #3 reverse-tooth
- Drill with bits: assorted
- Buffing wheel (optional)
- Sanders: belt (optional)
- Clean, soft paintbrush

The author used these products for the project. Substitute your choice of brands, tools, and materials as desired.

Wayne Fowler has been scrolling for over 30 years, first puzzles and then fretwork. Jacob Fowler has been drawing scroll saw designs since he was five (he drew a whale bank for his father, who collects whales). He got serious in his teens and has drawn well over a thousand designs since then. Together, Jacob and Wayne have published over 160 magazine articles, as well as the Woodworker's Pattern Book, available at Fox Chapel Publishing. They live in wood-rich Ontario, Canada, just outside Toronto. Find more of their work on Etsy at FantasiesISaw.

Easy Intarsia Snowman

All it takes to bring Frosty to life are a few small offcuts

By Brad Eklund and Hazel Trinidad

Christmas is a time of family, friends, and memories. Nostalgia is everywhere! One of those nostalgic memories we like to share with our kids is watching Christmas classics. Top of the list is, of course, *Frosty the Snowman*! It was after watching the classic cartoon that we designed this snowman ornament.

Cutting

Make five copies of the pattern: one for each kind of wood, plus a master copy for reference. Apply the patterns to their respective pieces of wood with repositionable spray adhesive, and then drill the ⅛" (3mm) holes for the eyes and buttons. Cut out all the pieces on a scroll saw. The great thing about this design is that most segments fit together easily, but if needed, use the saw to make minor fit adjustments. Remove the patterns.

Shaping

Shaping this project is straightforward. Give the body and head a slight round over with a rotary tool (using a ½" [13mm] sanding drum) to give them a bulbous look. Bring the branch arms down slightly lower than the body. Round the nose, but keep it higher than the head and scarf pieces so it protrudes out further. Thin down the two smaller scarf segments on the left side so they're slightly thinner than the rest of the scarf. Round the hat, tapering it down at the top. Use the edge of a ¼" (6mm) sanding drum to add the groove details to the hat, and add branch details using the same method. Sand everything smooth with 220-grit sandpaper. Round over and woodburn the tip of a ⅛" (3mm) dowel, and then cut it to length on the scroll saw for the eyes and buttons.

Assembling and Finishing

Now that everything is cut and shaped, it's time to glue all the segments together. Once the glue is dry, flatten the back side of the intarsia on a belt sander. Wipe off dust with a tack cloth, and then glue and clamp the entire thing to your backing material of choice. Once dry, carefully cut the backing flush to the intarsia on the scroll saw by trace cutting around the perimeter. *Note: Alternatively, you could trace the outline of the intarsia on the backing material and cut the backer by itself, staying just inside the line.* Spray with clear satin lacquer and let dry. Attach a hanger, screw eye and string, or other hardware of choice and display.

Easy Intarsia Snowman Pattern

R .... Red wood such as red heart
O ...... Orange wood such as chakte viga
L .... Light wood such as maple
D ...... Dark wood such as walnut

Materials & Tools

Materials
- Red wood, such as redheart, ½" (1.3cm) thick: hat and scarf, 2" (5.1cm) square
- Orange wood, such as chakte viga, ½" (1.3cm) thick: nose, ½" (1.3cm) square
- Light wood, such as maple, ½" (1.3cm) thick: body and head, 2" x 3" (5.1cm x 7.6cm)
- Dark wood, such as walnut, ½" (1.3cm) thick: arms, 1" (2.5cm) square
- Tempered hardboard, ⅛" (3mm) thick: backer, approx. 3" x 3¼" (7.6cm x 8.3cm)
- Spray adhesive: repositionable
- Sandpaper: 220-grit
- Dowel, ⅛" (3mm) thick: eyes and buttons, approx. 3" (7.6cm) long
- Tack cloth
- Lacquer: clear satin
- Wood glue

Tools
- Scroll saw with blades: #5 MGT
- Drill with bit: ⅛" (3mm)
- Sander: belt
- Rotary tool with bits: ¼" (6mm), ½" (13mm) sanding drum
- Clamps: small spring
- Woodburner with nib

The author used these products for the project. Substitute your choice of brands, tools, and materials as desired.

Brad Eklund and Hazel Trinidad have been creating scroll saw art for the last seven years. They have always been fascinated by the beauty and intricacies of wildlife and nature in general. Brad has a degree in horticulture, while Hazel has a degree in wildlife. They live and work next to a nature preserve in coastal North Carolina. Find more of their work on Etsy at EntwoodDesigns.

Poinsettia Box

Create a beautiful vessel with easy compound-cutting, wood veneer, and a little patience

By Carole Rothman

For a bright splash of color in winter, you can't beat the poinsettia plant (*Euphorbia pulcherrima*). Its striking beauty comes from colored bracts, which are modified leaves that last far longer than petals. The center of the poinsettia contains the actual flowers, which are tiny and yellow. Called cyathia, they provide an attractive contrast.

Creating flowers from wood is one of my passions, and I was curious to see how realistic a poinsettia I could make. Many patterns later, I was satisfied with the results. Since poinsettias are associated with Christmas, I designed a 12-sided box, complete with green veneer ribbons, to complement the bright red bracts.

This project is not difficult but does require patience. The veneer ribbons need careful placement, and painting the tiny balls to look like cyathia requires good tweezers and a steady hand. Once completed, however, its festive drama makes it worth the effort.

Check out our feature on Carole, page 68.

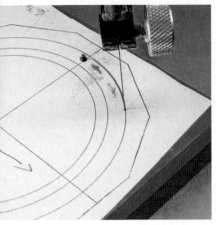

Getting Started

Mark the top edge of each blank. Cover the wood for the box body with blue painter's tape. Attach the box pattern; transfer the top mark to the pattern. Drill a blade-entry hole just inside circle A. Insert a #7 blade and cut out the box center, cutting just inside the line. Save the pattern from the center for use in Step 4. Next, use a spindle sander and 2" (5.1cm) spindle to sand the circle to the cut line. Sand away any fuzzies on the lower edge by hand.

A spindle sander works great for smoothing circular shapes.

MAKING THE BOX

1 **Attach the box bottom.** Sand the upper surface of the wood for the box bottom to 240-grit, and then glue that piece to the underside of the box body. Be sure to match the top edges of both pieces. Clamp, let dry five minutes, and then remove any glue squeeze-out from the inside of the box. Let dry thoroughly. Then cut just to the outside edge of the 12-sided cutting line. Use a belt sander to sand to that line.

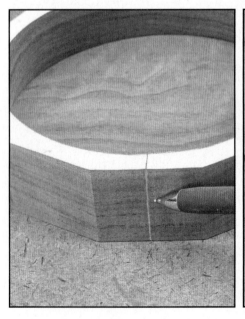
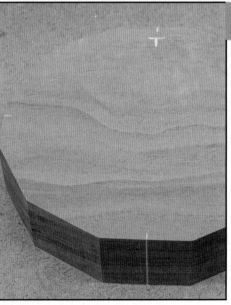

2 **Mark the locations of the ribbon pieces.** Use a square to transfer the four location lines on the pattern to the sides of the box body. Extend these lines onto the underside. Remove the pattern and label the top edge on both upper and lower surfaces.

> **TIP**
>
> ### MATCH THE GRAIN
>
> *For the most attractive appearance for the box, orient the wood for the lid, top, body, and bottom to obtain the best matches of grain and color. Mark the top edge of each piece to preserve this orientation.*

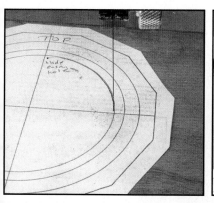

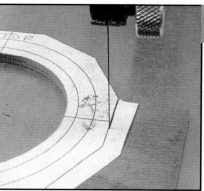

3 **Cut the box top.** Attach a second copy of the box pattern to the upper side of the wood for the top of the box, and then sand the underside of the wood to 220-grit. Drill a blade-entry hole just inside the cut line for circle C. Use a #3 blade to cut around the circle, cutting just inside the line. Remove the pattern and discard the cutout. Use the spindle sander to sand the center opening to the line. Then cut just to the outside edge of the 12-sided cutting line. Use the belt sander to sand to that line. Remove the pattern, transfer the top mark to the wood, then set the piece aside until Step 5.

4 **Cut the lid.** Attach the lid pattern that you saved earlier to the ⅛" (3mm) piece of walnut. Mark the center point deeply with an awl. This will guide the placement of the ribbon in Step 10. Use a #3 blade to cut around circle B, cutting just to the outside of the line. Sand to the line with the belt sander. Remove the pattern to save for the lid liner. Use a pneumatic drum with a 120-grit sleeve to bevel the top edge of the lid slightly, and then round it into a smooth curve. Use a 220-grit sleeve to refine the curve, and then finish by hand sanding with 220-grit sandpaper.

5 **Cut the lid liner.** Draw a diagonal line on the 4¾" (12.1cm) square of wood, and then cut the line to create two triangles. Smooth the cut edges on the belt sander. Invert one of the triangles, then apply a thin line of CA glue to one of the cut edges. Press the edges together and hold until set. Allow the piece dry. Draw a second diagonal across the uncut corners and repeat the process. Sand both sides until the piece lies flat and both faces are smooth. Attach the pattern saved from Step 4, using the awl to center it on the blank. Cut just to the outside of circle C, and then sand to the line with the belt sander. Place the box top from Step 3 on a flat surface. Place the lid liner in the opening and rotate it completely around. It should move freely without binding. If it binds and you can't locate the source, compare the lid and top openings with a copy of the pattern to see where corrections should be made. Sand any problematic areas in tiny increments, using the belt sander for the lid liner, and the spindle sander for the opening of the box top. Check the fit after each increment to avoid excessive play.

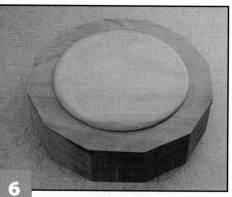

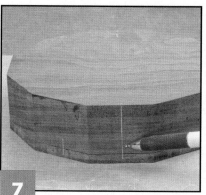

6 **Prepare the lid assembly.** Place a loop of blue painter's tape in the middle of the lid underside. Center the lid liner and press it down firmly to set the tape loop. Place the unit in the opening of the box top. The lid should be centered in the box and rotate freely all around. Set it aside until Step 9.

7 **Glue on the box top.** Apply a sealer coat of shellac to the inside of the box body and underside of the box top, avoiding the gluing surfaces. Sand lightly with 320-grit sandpaper when dry. Vacuum away the dust. Invert the box body on the box top. Adjust the pieces for the best alignment; mark the positions so you can realign the box easily. Apply glue to the box body and attach the top piece. Clamp and let dry. Secure the box in a bench vise, and then use a mouse or other small sander to sand the 12 sides smooth; all should be of equal length.

8

Bevel the box top. Set the belt sander table to 45°. Draw lines on the sides of the box, each located ⅛" (3mm) down from the top edge. Invert the box and sand just to the line. Use a pneumatic drum to soften the edges of the bevel; you can also continue the shaping into a soft curve. Then use the drum just to soften the edges of the bottom, the sides, and the upper edge of the center opening. Hand-sand the entire box to 220-grit.

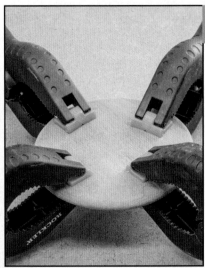

9

Complete the lid assembly. Insert the taped lid assembly from Step 6 into the box opening to confirm that it is centered and rotates freely. Remove and invert the lid. Mark the placement of the liner at several points around the circumference. Separate the pieces and remove the tape. Apply a thin coat of wood glue to the liner, keeping it about ⅛" (3mm) from the edges. Using the placement marks, position the liner on the underside of the lid. Press down firmly to set the bond, and then reinsert the unit to verify the positioning. If it is off-center, slide the liner slightly to correct. Remove the lid unit. Place four strong clamps around the circumference to prevent cupping. Let dry fully before removing clamps. *Note: Wood glue with a quick grab, such as Weldbond®, lets you slide the wood to make minor adjustments without disturbing the bond.*

ADDING THE RIBBONS

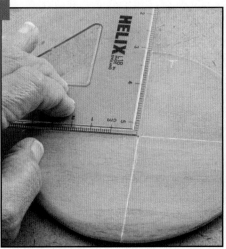

10

Draw location lines for the ribbons. Locate the marks on the underside of the box and use a straight edge and square to extend the lines up the sides and across the top. Then place the lid on the box in its correct orientation. Use a straightedge to draw a horizontal line across the center of the lid. It should pass through the awl mark in the center and be continuous with the lines on the box. Remove the lid and use the square to draw a second line that is perpendicular to the first and runs through the center awl mark. Extend the ends of the lines on the lid to its bottom and underside. Then replace the lid on the box. The lid and box lines should be continuous with each other. If not, adjust the lines on the box to match the lid.

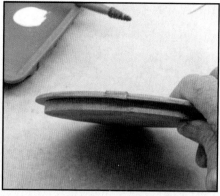

11 Cut the ribbons. Use an X-ACTO® knife, metal straightedge, and self-healing mat to cut the ribbon strips. All are ½" (1.3cm) wide, cut across the grain for flexibility, and are trimmed to size after being glued into place. You'll need two 5½" (14cm) strips for the lid, and four 3" (7.6cm) strips for the box top and sides. Cut some extras in case of breakage.

12 Glue on the lid ribbons. The lid strips are sized to overhang the outer edges of the lid and will be trimmed after gluing. Start by applying a thin, even layer of wood glue to one of the strips. The glue should cover only the section going over the flat part of the lid, leaving the ends at each side bare. Use the pencil marks on the lid underside as a guide for centering the strip on one of the lines. Press down firmly to secure the bond. Apply CA glue to the areas of the strip that will cover the edges of the lid. Press the strip firmly against the lid at these areas until the glue sets. Remove any glue squeeze-out at the sides of the ribbon with a toothpick and damp paper towel. Use an X-ACTO® knife to trim the overhang flush with the bottom of the lid. Cut the remaining lid strip in half and repeat this procedure for the two shorter segments. Soften the edges at the ends of the ribbons with sandpaper to keep the veneer from snagging.

13 Glue on the box ribbons. Place the lid on the box. The lines on the box should align with the center of the lid ribbons; adjust the lines, if needed. Remove the lid and elevate the box. Trim the four side strips so they extend from slightly into the box opening to slightly below the lower edge. Glue them one at a time, starting at the center opening. Press firmly to prevent air bubbles, and to secure the bond. Trim the ends flush when the glue has set. Replace the lid briefly after gluing each box strip to check the alignment. When all strips are glued, sand away any glue residue at the sides of the ribbons, and then sand all ribbon edges—top, bottom, and sides—to a slight bevel to prevent snagging. Sand the faces of the strips to 240. Carefully restore the awl mark to the center of the lid and deepen it. This will be needed in Step 19.

MAKING THE BRACTS

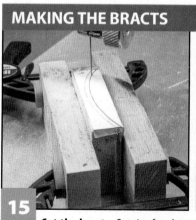

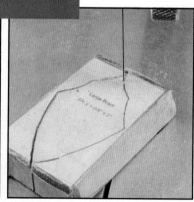

14 Complete the box and lid. Use blue painter's tape to mask a 2" (5.1cm) circle in the center of the lid. Apply a sealer coat of shellac to the box exterior and both sides of the lid. Remove any visible dried glue, and then sand the box and lid progressively to 320-grit. Remove all sanding dust and apply two light coats of gloss spray lacquer.

15 Cut the bracts. Cut six of each pattern. This gives you one extra, just in case. For each, sharply crease the pattern on the line dividing the top and side faces. Attach the pattern with repositionable adhesive. Start by cutting the side profile. Use a #7 blade with support blocks and small clamps, or a jig, for stability. After cutting that side, tape the pieces back together with clear packaging tape and cut the front profile.

16 **Sand the bracts.** For the large and medium bracts, use the belt sander to smooth the lower edges, and the pneumatic drum with medium grit sleeve to smooth the edges of the upper indentations. Use the pneumatic drum with a fine grit sleeve to refine the top and bottom surfaces, and to round over the upper edges for a delicate appearance without fragility. For the small bracts, use a small pneumatic drum for all shaping. Finish sanding by hand to 320-grit.

17 **Paint the bracts.** Mark the gluing areas with light pencil lines. For large bracts, the gluing area extends ¾" (1.9cm) up from the tip for the back surface and ⁷⁄₁₆" (1.1cm) for the front. For medium bracts, they extend ½" (1.3cm) for the back and ¼" (6mm) for the front. For small bracts, they extend ³⁄₈" (1cm) for the back only. Apply two or three coats of paint, avoiding the gluing areas. If your paint has a flat finish, try buffing a test piece very gently with a 320-grit sanding mop to obtain a soft sheen. You can also apply extra coats of gloss spray lacquer when finishing.

18 **Paint the cyathia.** You need six, but prepare extras; the tiny balls are hard to control. Working one at a time, hold the ball in position with locking pliers with the jaws covered with masking tape. Use a #54 drill bit to drill a hole deep enough to hold a toothpick securely. Insert the toothpick and use a small brush to paint the cyathia a pale yellow-green. When dry, dip it into thinned yellow paint to form a circle on top.

19 **Attach the bracts.** Place the lid on the box in the correct orientation, with lid and box ribbons continuous with each other. Attach a loop of masking tape, sticky side out, to the bottom gluing area of each of the five large bracts. Arrange them around the center awl mark. The top bract should be aligned with the top lid and box ribbons. Space the remaining bracts evenly. Press the bracts firmly into place to set their position, and then glue them on one at a time. Start by removing the tape loop from the top bract. Use a toothpick to spread CA glue on the gluing area, keeping the glue away from the edges. Press the bract into place, pressing down firmly at the end until the glue has set. Next, glue the adjacent bracts into place, and then the two at the bottom. When this layer has set, glue on the medium bracts. Center each between two bracts of the first layer, with the pointed end near the awl mark. For the small bracts, use tape loops to position them between the medium bracts. Their tips should meet at the awl mark. If the fit is too tight, use a small sanding block to sand the sides of the gluing areas until the bracts can meet. Glue them into place between the bracts of the second layer.

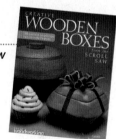

20 **Finish the box.** Flatten the undersides of six cyathia with a sanding block. Holding one cyathium with tweezers, apply a small amount of CA glue to its bottom. Press it into place directly over the awl mark and let it set. To preview areas where bare wood might be visible, place the remaining five cyathia, without glue, between the small bracts. If you see any bare spots, remove the cyathia and paint those areas with a small brush. When dry, glue the remaining five cyathia into place between the small bracts. Apply one or two light coats of gloss spray lacquer to the flower and lid, and then check the box body to see if additional coats are needed.

Materials & Tools

Materials
- Walnut, 1 1⁄16" (2.7cm) thick: box body, 7" (17.8cm) square
- Walnut, ¼" (6mm) thick: 2 each box top and bottom, 7" (17.8cm) square
- Walnut, ⅛" (3mm) thick: box lid, 5½" (14cm) square
- Walnut, ¼" (6mm) thick: lid liner, 4¾" (12.1cm) square
- Aspen, ¾" (1.9cm) thick: large bracts, 6 each 1¾" x 3" (4.5cm x 7.6cm)
- Aspen, ¾" (1.9cm) thick: medium bracts, 6 each 1¾" x 2¾" (4.5cm x 7cm)
- Aspen, ¾" (1.9cm) thick: small bracts, 6 each 1¼" x 2" (3.2cm x 5.1cm)
- Dyed green veneer for ribbons
- Wooden balls: 10 each ¼" (6mm)-dia.

- Pencil
- Sandpaper: assorted grits
- Wood glue, such as Weldbond®
- CA glue, such as Titebond Instant Bond Medium
- Spray adhesive: repositionable
- Tape: blue painter's, clear packaging, masking
- Toothpicks
- Acrylic paints: green, yellow, white
- Gel stain, such as Unicorn Spit: Molly red pepper
- Shellac
- Lacquer: spray gloss
- Paper towels

Tools
- Scroll saw with blades: #3, #7
- Clamps: assorted

- Drill press with bits: ⅛" (3mm) and #54
- Sanders: belt, spindle, pneumatic drum, mouse
- Self-healing mat
- X-ACTO® knife with blades
- Metal straightedge
- Right angle square
- Locking pliers
- Paintbrushes: assorted
- Tweezers
- Awl
- Sanding block

The author used these products for the project. Substitute your choice of brands, tools, and materials as desired.

Patterns for the ***POINSETTIA BOX*** are in the pullout section.

Carole Rothman of Pawling, N.Y., is a retired psychologist and college professor. She is also an award-winning cake decorator. Visit Carole online at scrollsawbowls.blogspot.com. You'll find her books, Creative Wooden Boxes from the Scroll Saw *and* Scroll Saw Wooden Bowls: Revised & Expanded Edition, *at foxchapelpublishing.com.*

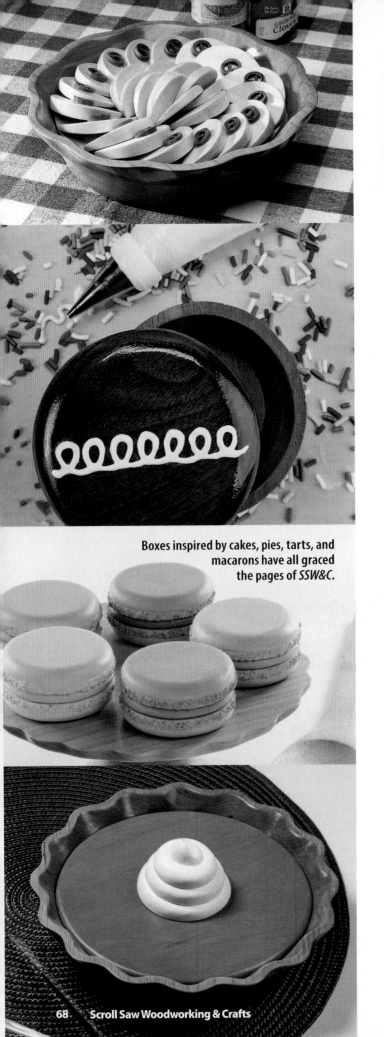

Piece of Cake

Carole Rothman talks baking, box making, and the value of constant experimentation

By Kaylee Schofield

Boxes inspired by cakes, pies, tarts, and macarons have all graced the pages of *SSW&C*.

arole Rothman is the sort of person who will offer an incisive project critique and then, in the same breath, send you her favorite recipe for Morning Glory muffins. But these actions aren't so diametrically opposed: Carole's background as a professional baker is part of what makes her wooden creations so delectable.

Her love for making things by hand started even earlier, though. A native Manhattanite, Carole began sewing her own clothes at age ten, in part inspired by solo subway rides around the local art scene. In later years, she would study music and the mind, eventually earning her Ph.D. in clinical psychology. Then, always eager to take on more, she began baking unique cakes.

"Some replicated objects as diverse as attaché cases and baskets of fruit, while others were decorated with ribbons, bows, or flowers, all made from sugar paste," Carole said. Her skills even found their way into how-to articles for a cake decorating magazine.

A simple bowl from Carole's early woodworking days.

A more recent work uses inlaid dowels to create polka dots in a purpleheart bowl.

After joining a community woodshop, Carole began applying these skills of precision and design to baskets and boxes, often inspired by desserts. Instead of a cake decorator's flower nail, she used a scroll saw to create 3-D petals (like those in her Poinsettia Box on page 61); for smoothing contours, she swapped the cake scraper for a spindle sander. Exhilarated by the possibilities natural wood grain had to offer, Carole developed a process of careful experimentation that holds true for her designs today: each prototype undergoes a rigorous period of "editing" for aesthetics, fit, and structural integrity.

Her partner, Joe (a woodworker in his own right), concurs. "Carole loves word and number puzzles of various types," he said. "When she's determined to solve one, she spares no effort."

So it follows that, while preparing one of her many surprise constructions—a Hamsa box (religious symbol for protection from darkness) given to a friend with chronic illness, the Man's Best Friend sculpture (issue #86) for a dog lover she knows—Carole seems to retreat from time altogether, the converted garage bay serving as her lab, brightly lit and packed with sanders.

Sometimes her gifts come in the form of advice: Dave Van Ess, a fellow bowl maker and longtime collaborator (see his project on page 70), says she helped him develop a software program to aid woodworkers with bowl design calculations. Likewise, when Carole's book, *Wooden Bowls from the Scroll Saw,* came out in 2010, Dave traded a piece of redwood lace burl for a signed copy.

"When it came, the first thing I did was run out to get materials to build a bowl press from the book," he said. "I mean, I stopped reading and went to buy materials. I have never done that before or since."

Carole's other designs demonstrate the same out-of-the-box thinking that inspired readers like Dave a decade ago. For one, she doesn't just use plain hardwood: to simulate "feet" on her macaron boxes (shown at left), she glued wood shavings around the rim; to create perfectly sized "sprinkles" for sugar cookie ornaments, she painstakingly scrolled small pieces of dyed veneer and then applied them with tweezers. She even "had a brief love affair with Corian," which was short-lived due to the powdery mess it made in her shop. However, as a self-dubbed perfectionist, Carole rarely shies away from a challenge—which has garnered admiration from a group Dave calls "the Carole Heads."

"If I am different in approach from her in an article, the Carole Heads ask why I did it that way," he chuckled. "They ask if I am saying Carole is wrong. I say, *No, I just do it differently.* Carole responds that she likes her way better. I'm never going to win this argument, am I, Carole?"

One thing they can agree on, though, is the importance of a can-do attitude in the workshop, summed up perfectly by Carole's motto: "Everything will not always work out exactly as you want it to, but that should never stop you from trying."

Find more of Carole's work at scrollsawbowls.blogspot.com.

Carole's proudest woodworking achievement, this box, placed third at a large woodworking contest in 2007 and encouraged her to begin authoring project articles for *SSW&C* magazine.

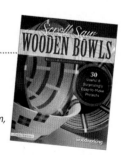

Tiniest Cabin
CONSTRUCTION SET

Tiny homes are a trend these days, but this wee log cabin has them all beat

By Dave Van Ess

This fun toy is easy to cut but requires the ability to make straight lines and corners. You can master these skills with just a little practice. When cutting is complete, you will have 36 pieces that can be assembled into a log cabin measuring 3 ¾" (9.5cm) wide, 3 ½" (8.9cm) deep, and 3 ¾" (9.5cm) tall with a chimney. It's the perfect log cabin for a mini Abe Lincoln!

Getting Started

Photocopy the cabin and roof slat patterns. Cover both blanks with blue painter's tape (or any appropriate tape). Use repositionable spray adhesive to attach the roof slat pattern to the ⅛" (3mm) blank, and then attach the cabin pattern to the ¼" (6mm) blank. Smooth out any air bubbles or creases.

Cutting

Use a #2 skip-tooth blade to make all the horizontal and vertical straight cuts. You will end up with six roof slats, one front header, one windowsill, one front plate, one back plate, four back slats, eight side slats, two roof gables, three chimney pieces, and 13 stubs (two spares).

Make the corner cuts on the three chimney pieces. Lightly sand them with 150-grit paper, and then remove dust with a soft cloth. Glue and assemble the chimney. Clamp and set aside to dry. By the time you finish the rest of the cuts, the glue will be dry and the chimney will be ready to place on top of the cabin.

Cut the gables, and then cut all the notches. There are a lot of notches, but they cut easily with a #2 blade. Take your time because all the cabin "logs" need to be able to fit smoothly into each other for assembly.

Finishing

When all pieces are cut, lightly sand them with 150-grit sandpaper, and then remove dust with a soft cloth. To finish the wood, I give all the pieces a quick dunk in diluted mineral oil, which is half mineral oil and half mineral spirits. Let the pieces dry, then wipe off any excess finish with a clean rag.

> Patterns for the ***TINIEST CABIN CONSTRUCTION SET*** are in the pullout section.

Materials & Tools

Materials
- Baltic birch plywood, ¼" (6mm) thick: cabin pieces, 4" x 10" (10.2cm x 25.4cm)
- Baltic birch plywood, ⅛" (3mm) thick: roof slats, 4" (10.2cm) square
- Tape: blue painter's
- Spray adhesive
- Sandpaper: 150-grit
- Soft cloth
- Finish, such as mineral oil or mineral spirits, acrylic paints (optional)
- Wood glue
- Box of choice: 1" x 4" x 4" (2.5cm x 10.2cm x 10.2cm)

Tools
- Scroll saw with blade: #2 skip-tooth
- Spring clamps

The author used these products for the project. Substitute your choice of brands, tools, and materials as desired.

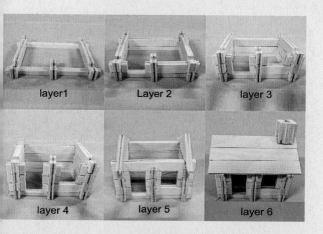

layer1   Layer 2   layer 3

layer 4   layer 5   layer 6

Assembling the Cabin

The cabin is composed of five layers plus a roof and chimney. Each layer is a criss-cross that starts with pieces aligned left to right followed by pieces placed on top aligned front to back.

- Layer 1 has a front plate and a back plate on which is placed a side slat, a stub, and another side slat.
- Layer 2 starts with back slat, stub, and a windowsill. Place a side slat, stub, and another side slat on top of that.
- Layer 3 starts with a back slat and three stubs. Place a side slat, a stub, and another side slat on top of that.
- Layer 4 is completed just like the previous layer.
- Layer 5 starts with a back slat and a front header with two roof gables on top.
- Add the roof slats and chimney to complete.

TIPS

GREAT KID'S GIFT

This little cabin makes a great gift for children five and up (the smallest pieces are not suitable for very young children). I often leave all the wood unfinished so recipients can paint it with the colors of their choice. This is a fun project for crafty kids, and I recommend painting with simple acrylics.

STORING THE PIECES

I found nice boxes online for packaging and storing the cabin pieces. Look for inside dimensions of 1" x 4" x 4" (2.5cm x 10.2cm x 10.2cm). The ones I found cost only 50 cents each when bought in a pack of 50.

Dave Van Ess is a retired engineer living in Chandler, Ariz. He has been woodworking for 45 years and scrolling for 35 years. He is a past president of Arizona Woodworkers (a greater Phoenix area woodworking club), and likes teaching woodworking to young people. He promptly builds whatever his two grandkids request and lets them use his nail gun when their nana isn't around!

STATEMENT OF OWNERSHIP

Statement of Ownership, Management and Circulation Published in accordance with US Postal Service regulations. 1) Publication Title: Scroll Saw Woodworking & Crafts. 2) Publication No.: 1532-5091. 3) Filing Date: August 28, 2023. 4) Issue Frequency: Quarterly. 5) Number of Issues published annually: 4. 6) Annual subscription price: $29.99. 7) Complete mailing address of known office of publication: Fox Chapel Publishing Co., Inc., 903 Square Street, Mount Joy, PA 17552-1911– Lancaster County. 8) Same. 9) Full Name and complete mailing address of Publisher, Editor, and Managing Editor: Publisher – Alan Giagnocavo, 903 Square Street, Mount Joy, PA 17552-1911, Lancaster County. Editor – Kaylee Schofield, 903 Square Street, Mount Joy, PA 17552-1911, Lancaster County. 10) Owner: Alan Giagnocavo, 903 Square Street, Mount Joy, PA 17552-1911, Lancaster County. 11) Known Bondholders: none 12) Tax Status: Has not changed during preceding 12 months. 13) Publication Title: Scroll Saw Woodworking & Crafts. 14) Issue Date for circulation data below: 03/28/2023. 15) Extent and Nature of Circulation – Average No. Copies Each Issue During Preceding 12 months/Actual Copies of Single Issue Published Nearest to filing Date: A. Total Number of Copies (net press run): 29,527/26,177. B. (1) Paid Outside County Mail Subscriptions: 11,592/11,157. B. (2) Paid In-County Subscriptions: 0/0. B. (3) Sales Through Dealers and Carriers, Street Vendors, Counter Sales and Other Non-USPS Paid Distribution: 4,920/4,314. B. (4) Other Classes Mailed Through the USPS: 138/80. C. Total Paid Circulation: 15,650/15,551. D. Free Distribution by Mail (Samples, Complimentary, and Other Free) (1) Outside-County: 30/32 (2) In-County: 0/0 (3) Other Classes Mailed Through the USPS: 580/563. (4) Outside the Mail (carriers or other means): 109/75. E. Total Free or Nominal Rate Distribution: 719/670. F. Total Distribution: 17,369/16,221. G. Copies Not Distributed: 12,158/9,956. H. Total: 29,527/26,177. I. Percentage Paid and/or Requested Circulation: 95.9%/95.9% 16.) Total Circulation includes Electronic Copies: No 17) Publication Required. Will be printed in the 09/26/2023 issue of this publication. 18) Kaylee Schofield, Editor – 8/28/2023.

FOX HUNT

Fred Langton of University Place, Wash., and Mary Payne of Pine City, Minn., were randomly drawn from the readers who located the fox in our last issue (Fall 2023, Issue #92). The fox was moon gazing in Sue Mey's Howling Wolf Fretwork article on page 63.

Find the fox in this issue, and tell us the page number and location. Two readers randomly selected from all correct replies will receive a $25 Fox Chapel Publishing gift certificate. Entries must be received by Nov. 22, 2023, to be eligible. *Note: The contest fox is an outline drawing that would face left if its feet were on the "ground" (other foxes appearing in SSW&C don't count).*

Send your entry to SSW&C, Attn: Find the Fox, 903 Square Street, Mount Joy, PA 17552 or enter online at scrollsawer.com.

Layered Snowflake Ornaments

Contrasting woods add depth and body to these delicate designs

By Keith Fenton
Cut by Rolf Beuttenmuller

Patterns for the *LAYERED SNOWFLAKE ORNAMENTS* are in the pullout section.

Create a multitude of unique designs from these snowflake patterns. Stack cutting this project will yield a blizzard of them in no time!

Getting Started

Photocopy the patterns, and then sand both sides of the wood with a hand-held orbital sander. Start with 100-grit sandpaper, progressing to 150. Clean all dust with a soft cloth.

Affix the pattern to the wood in your usual manner. Then use a small bit in a drill press to drill the entry holes for the interior cuts and the hanging holes. After drilling, sand the backs of the blanks so they lay perfectly flat as you cut.

Cutting

Use a scroll saw with a #2/0 reverse-tooth blade to cut out the designs, beginning with the interior cuts. After cutting, use a sanding block or orbital sander to carefully remove burrs. You can start with 150-grit paper and finish with 220. Use a sanding stick to remove any burrs that remain, and then remove dust with a soft cloth.

Assembling and Finishing

Use clear-drying wood glue on the backs of the front pieces to glue them onto the backers. A small, water-dampened brush is helpful for spreading glue on the thin front pieces. Line up the two layers carefully and weight them with a paperweight as the glue dries.

Spray the snowflakes on both sides with several light coats of a finish of your choice, allowing ample drying time between coats. For a smoother finish, you can sand the surface lightly by hand with 400- or 600-grit paper. Clean off the dust before applying a last coat, if desired. Allow the finish to dry, and then attach a decorative string or cord.

Materials & Tool

Materials

- Wood, such as yellow heart, red heart, purpleheart, cherry, holly, butternut, or Baltic birch plywood, ⅛" (3mm) thick: front layer, 7" x 12" (17.8cm x 30.5cm)
- Wood, such as yellow heart, red heart, purpleheart, cherry, holly, butternut, or Baltic birch plywood, ⅛" (3mm) thick: back layer, 7" x 12" (17.8cm x 30.5cm)
- Glue: spray adhesive; wood: clear drying
- Tape: blue painter's or masking, clear packaging (optional)
- Sandpaper: assorted grits to 600
- Soft cloth
- Sealer, such as Minwax lacquer spray or polyurethane spray
- Small cord or decorative string

Tools

- Scroll saw with blades: #2/0 reverse-tooth
- Drill press with bits: small
- Sander: orbital
- Sanding block (optional)
- Sanding stick (optional)
- Paper weight
- Small paintbrush

The author used these products for the project. Substitute your choice of brands, tools, and materials as desired.

Keith Fenton has been designing scroll saw patterns for several years alongside his partner, Sheila Landry. Together they have contributed patterns and articles to several woodworking and painting magazines and e-zines. You can visit their website at sheilalandrydesign com to see their entire selection of patterns (including fr samples). If you have any questions about this project, you can reach Keith at sheilalandrydesigns@gmail.com

Rolf Beuttenmuller started scrolling in 2004 after his wi June, bought him a scroll saw for his birthday. He joined a local club and enjoys new and challenging projects. His motto is, "I don't know that I can't, therefore I can." Rolf retired from Brookhaven National Lab after 34 yea of designing and building special devices for high energ and photon science research. He lives in Bellport, N.Y.

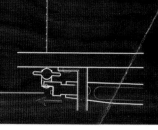